I0020809

RECONNAISSANCE 101
FOOTPRINTING & INFORMATION GATHERING

ETHICAL HACKERS BIBLE TO COLLECT DATA ABOUT TARGET SYSTEMS

4 BOOKS IN 1

BOOK 1
RECONNAISSANCE 101: A BEGINNER'S GUIDE TO FOOTPRINTING & INFORMATION GATHERING

BOOK 2
MASTERING FOOTPRINTING: ADVANCED INFORMATION GATHERING STRATEGIES FOR ETHICAL HACKERS

BOOK 3
THE ETHICAL HACKER'S FIELD GUIDE TO TARGET DATA ACQUISITION

BOOK 4
RECONNAISSANCE PRO: THE ULTIMATE HANDBOOK FOR ELITE INFORMATION GATHERERS

ROB BOTWRIGHT

Copyright © 2023 by Rob Botwright
All rights reserved. No part of this book may be reproduced or transmitted in any form or by any means, electronic or mechanical, including photocopying, recording, or by any information storage and retrieval system, without permission in writing from the publisher.

Published by Rob Botwright
Library of Congress Cataloging-in-Publication Data
ISBN 978-1-83938-549-0
Cover design by Rizzo

Disclaimer

The contents of this book are based on extensive research and the best available historical sources. However, the author and publisher make no claims, promises, or guarantees about the accuracy, completeness, or adequacy of the information contained herein. The information in this book is provided on an "as is" basis, and the author and publisher disclaim any and all liability for any errors, omissions, or inaccuracies in the information or for any actions taken in reliance on such information.

The opinions and views expressed in this book are those of the author and do not necessarily reflect the official policy or position of any organization or individual mentioned in this book. Any reference to specific people, places, or events is intended only to provide historical context and is not intended to defame or malign any group, individual, or entity.

The information in this book is intended for educational and entertainment purposes only. It is not intended to be a substitute for professional advice or judgment. Readers are encouraged to conduct their own research and to seek professional advice where appropriate.

Every effort has been made to obtain necessary permissions and acknowledgments for all images and other copyrighted material used in this book. Any errors or omissions in this regard are unintentional, and the author and publisher will correct them in future editions.

TABLE OF CONTENTS – BOOK 1 - RECONNAISSANCE 101: A BEGINNER'S GUIDE TO FOOTPRINTING & INFORMATION GATHERING

TABLE OF CONTENTS – BOOK 2 - MASTERING FOOTPRINTING: ADVANCED INFORMATION GATHERING STRATEGIES FOR ETHICAL HACKERS

TABLE OF CONTENTS – BOOK 3 - THE ETHICAL HACKER'S FIELD GUIDE TO TARGET DATA ACQUISITION

TABLE OF CONTENTS – BOOK 4 - RECONNAISSANCE PRO: THE ULTIMATE HANDBOOK FOR ELITE INFORMATION GATHERERS

Introduction

In the ever-evolving landscape of cybersecurity, reconnaissance stands as the cornerstone of every successful endeavor. The art of gathering information, understanding systems, and navigating the digital terrain with precision has never been more critical. As the digital realm expands, so do the challenges and opportunities for those who wish to safeguard it.

Welcome to "RECONNAISSANCE 101: Footprinting & Information Gathering," a comprehensive book bundle that unveils the secrets of ethical hacking and data acquisition. This four-volume collection is designed to guide you through the intricacies of reconnaissance, whether you're just starting your journey or looking to elevate your expertise to the highest levels.

Book 1 - "RECONNAISSANCE 101: A Beginner's Guide to Footprinting & Information Gathering" is your entry point into the captivating world of ethical hacking. Here, you'll embark on a journey that demystifies the fundamental concepts and techniques of reconnaissance. This volume lays the groundwork, ensuring that you have a solid foundation upon which to build your skills.

Book 2 - "Mastering Footprinting: Advanced Information Gathering Strategies for Ethical Hackers" takes you to the next level. As you progress through this volume, you'll discover advanced strategies and tactics used by ethical hackers to gather valuable data, all while staying in the shadows, undetected. This book is your gateway to mastering the art of footprinting.

Book 3 - "The Ethical Hacker's Field Guide to Target Data Acquisition" brings a laser focus to the crucial task of acquiring target-specific data. Here, you'll explore ethical methods for collecting information that is essential for ethical hackers in assessing vulnerabilities and potential exploits. This volume equips you with the skills needed to navigate the complexities of data acquisition.

Book 4 - "Reconnaissance Pro: The Ultimate Handbook for Elite Information Gatherers" catapults you to the highest echelons of reconnaissance expertise. Within its pages, you'll unravel the secrets of elite information gatherers, gaining insights into techniques that set apart the best in the field. This book is your passport to becoming a true master of reconnaissance.

Throughout this book bundle, we emphasize not only the technical aspects of reconnaissance but also the ethical considerations that guide ethical hackers. Responsible disclosure and collaboration with authorities are core principles that underscore the importance of ethical hacking in today's digital landscape.

As you dive into these volumes, remember that your journey is more than just acquiring knowledge; it's a commitment to ethical practices, responsible behavior, and making the digital world a safer place for all. The skills and principles you'll gain from "RECONNAISSANCE 101: Footprinting & Information Gathering" will serve as a strong foundation for your cybersecurity career.

Whether you're an aspiring ethical hacker looking to understand the fundamentals or an experienced professional seeking to enhance your reconnaissance abilities, this book bundle is tailored to meet your needs. We invite you to embark on this educational adventure, explore the world of reconnaissance, and unlock the potential to become a skilled and responsible guardian of the digital realm.

Join us in this journey of discovery, empowerment, and ethical hacking. Together, we'll explore the depths of "RECONNAISSANCE 101: Footprinting & Information Gathering" and equip you with the knowledge and tools to thrive in the dynamic world of cybersecurity.

BOOK 1
RECONNAISSANCE 101
A BEGINNER'S GUIDE TO FOOTPRINTING & INFORMATION GATHERING

ROB BOTWRIGHT

Chapter 1: Introduction to Reconnaissance

The importance of reconnaissance in cybersecurity cannot be overstated; it forms the foundation upon which effective defense and offense strategies are built.

Reconnaissance, often referred to as the first phase of the cyber attack lifecycle, plays a pivotal role in understanding potential targets and vulnerabilities.

This initial phase involves gathering information about the target, which could be an organization, network, or even an individual, with the intent of identifying weaknesses that can be exploited.

Reconnaissance is not exclusive to malicious actors; it is equally critical for cybersecurity professionals and ethical hackers who aim to safeguard systems and data.

By comprehensively understanding the significance of reconnaissance, individuals can better appreciate its role in the broader context of cybersecurity.

In essence, reconnaissance is the process of collecting data about a target, and it serves as the foundation upon which subsequent actions are based.

Without a thorough understanding of the target, it becomes challenging to formulate effective strategies to protect against cyber threats or to assess the security posture of a system.

One of the primary objectives of reconnaissance is to gather as much information as possible while remaining discreet and undetected.

This is crucial because the more an attacker knows about their target, the more likely they are to exploit vulnerabilities successfully.

At the same time, ethical hackers and cybersecurity professionals use reconnaissance to discover and address weaknesses before malicious actors can take advantage of them.

There are various techniques and methodologies employed in reconnaissance, ranging from passive information gathering to active probing of a target's systems.

Passive techniques involve collecting publicly available information, often referred to as Open Source Intelligence (OSINT), without directly interacting with the target.

This could include mining data from websites, social media profiles, or even online forums and discussion boards.

Active reconnaissance, on the other hand, involves actively probing a target's systems, often through techniques like scanning networks, probing for open ports, and identifying potential vulnerabilities.

In the realm of ethical hacking and cybersecurity, reconnaissance is an essential step in the process of vulnerability assessment and penetration testing.

Before attempting to exploit any vulnerabilities, ethical hackers must thoroughly understand the target environment to assess potential risks accurately.

It's essential to recognize that reconnaissance isn't limited to technical aspects alone.

Social engineering, another critical component of reconnaissance, focuses on manipulating human psychology to gather information or gain unauthorized access.

Through techniques like phishing, pretexting, and tailgating, attackers can exploit human trust and curiosity, making social engineering an indispensable part of reconnaissance.

Furthermore, reconnaissance extends beyond traditional networks into the realm of web applications and cloud services.

Web application reconnaissance involves identifying vulnerabilities in web applications that can be exploited to compromise data or gain unauthorized access.

Cloud reconnaissance is equally crucial, as organizations increasingly rely on cloud services for their data storage and processing needs.

In recent years, there has been a growing emphasis on the significance of deep and dark web reconnaissance.

The deep web consists of web pages not indexed by search engines, while the dark web is intentionally hidden and accessible only through specialized browsers.

These hidden parts of the internet are often associated with illegal activities, making them a significant concern for cybersecurity professionals.

Advanced reconnaissance techniques involve leveraging tools and automation to streamline the data collection process.

These tools can help in systematically gathering and analyzing information about a target, saving time and ensuring comprehensive coverage.

Another crucial aspect of reconnaissance is vulnerability assessment.

This entails identifying potential weaknesses in a target's systems or applications that could be exploited by attackers.

By conducting vulnerability assessments, organizations can proactively address security flaws before they are exploited.

As reconnaissance plays a central role in the broader cybersecurity landscape, it is imperative for both defenders and attackers to continually evolve their techniques.

Defenders must develop robust strategies to detect and mitigate reconnaissance attempts, while attackers continuously refine their methods to evade detection and gather more valuable information.

It is also essential to note that ethical considerations loom large in the world of reconnaissance.

The line between ethical hacking and malicious cyber activity can sometimes blur, highlighting the need for a strong ethical framework.

Ethical hackers adhere to a strict code of conduct, ensuring that their reconnaissance efforts are legal and conducted with the utmost integrity.

Furthermore, the legal landscape surrounding reconnaissance is complex and continually evolving.

Laws and regulations governing data privacy, cybersecurity, and hacking vary by jurisdiction, making it crucial for individuals and organizations to stay informed and compliant.

In summary, reconnaissance is the cornerstone of effective cybersecurity.

Understanding its importance, techniques, and ethical considerations is vital for individuals seeking to protect systems and data or to identify vulnerabilities in their security posture.

Whether you are a cybersecurity professional, an ethical hacker, or someone interested in safeguarding their digital presence, reconnaissance is a fundamental concept that forms the basis for informed and proactive decision-making in the world of cybersecurity.

Exploring the history and evolution of reconnaissance techniques provides valuable insights into the development of modern cybersecurity practices.

Reconnaissance, in various forms, has been a part of human conflict and espionage throughout history.

In ancient times, reconnaissance often involved sending scouts or spies to gather information about an enemy's movements, fortifications, and resources.

These early reconnaissance efforts were essential for military strategists to make informed decisions and gain a tactical advantage.

As societies advanced, so did the techniques of reconnaissance, which began to encompass a broader range of information-gathering methods.

The advent of the printing press in the 15th century revolutionized the dissemination of information, enabling intelligence to be collected and shared more widely.

During the World Wars of the 20th century, reconnaissance evolved significantly with the use of aerial photography and radio communications.

Aerial reconnaissance allowed for detailed mapping of enemy territory and the identification of military installations and troop movements.

Radio communications enabled real-time information sharing among military units, facilitating coordinated actions.

The Cold War era saw further advancements in reconnaissance techniques, particularly in the realm of signals intelligence (SIGINT).

Governments and intelligence agencies developed sophisticated methods to intercept and decipher encrypted communications, giving them a significant intelligence advantage.

The development of satellites further expanded reconnaissance capabilities. Satellites could provide high-resolution images and monitor activities worldwide.

These advancements in reconnaissance had military, political, and economic implications, with nations competing to gain access to the latest intelligence technologies.

The rise of the internet in the late 20th century ushered in a new era of reconnaissance, one that extended beyond the traditional realms of espionage and warfare.

With the internet, information became more accessible, and reconnaissance evolved to include digital footprints, online behaviors, and vulnerabilities.

Hackers and cybercriminals began to leverage digital reconnaissance to identify targets, gather sensitive information, and exploit vulnerabilities in computer systems. In response to these emerging threats, cybersecurity professionals and ethical hackers developed new techniques for reconnaissance.

Open Source Intelligence (OSINT) emerged as a critical component of modern reconnaissance, focusing on gathering publicly available information from online sources. OSINT tools and methodologies allowed security experts to assess the digital footprint of organizations and individuals, identifying potential weaknesses.

While reconnaissance was once primarily the domain of governments and intelligence agencies, it has become democratized in the digital age.

Individuals and organizations now have access to a wealth of information and tools to conduct their reconnaissance activities. However, with this accessibility comes increased responsibility, as the ethical and legal boundaries of reconnaissance must be carefully considered.

As technology continues to advance, so too will the field of reconnaissance.

The Internet of Things (IoT), artificial intelligence (AI), and machine learning are poised to revolutionize how information is collected and processed in the digital landscape.

AI-powered algorithms can analyze vast amounts of data to identify patterns and anomalies, assisting in the automated detection of vulnerabilities.

Additionally, the proliferation of IoT devices presents new opportunities and challenges for reconnaissance, as these devices generate valuable data and potential attack vectors.

In the context of cybersecurity, reconnaissance serves as the first line of defense against cyber threats.

By proactively identifying vulnerabilities and monitoring for suspicious activities, organizations can strengthen their security posture and mitigate potential risks.

Ethical hackers play a crucial role in this process, using reconnaissance techniques to assess the security of systems and applications.

They simulate real-world cyberattacks, identify weaknesses, and recommend remediation strategies to protect against malicious actors.

The evolution of reconnaissance techniques reflects the dynamic nature of cybersecurity.

In an interconnected world, where data is a valuable asset, staying ahead of potential threats requires constant adaptation and innovation.

Understanding the history and evolution of reconnaissance is not just a matter of historical curiosity but a vital aspect of navigating the complex and ever-changing landscape of digital security.

As individuals and organizations continue to rely on technology, the ability to conduct effective reconnaissance and protect against reconnaissance attempts remains paramount.

In summary, the history and evolution of reconnaissance techniques underscore its enduring significance in both military and cybersecurity contexts.

From ancient spies and scouts to modern cyber threats, reconnaissance has played a pivotal role in shaping strategies and defenses.

As technology continues to advance, the field of reconnaissance will evolve further, demanding continued vigilance and adaptation to meet the challenges of an interconnected world.

Chapter 2: Understanding Footprinting

Exploring the world of footprinting methods and tools is like embarking on a journey through the digital landscape, where information is the treasure, and knowledge is the map.

Footprinting, also known as reconnaissance, is the first step in the realm of cybersecurity—a journey that begins with understanding and gathering information about a target.

In this chapter, we'll delve into the fascinating world of footprinting methods and the diverse array of tools that have been developed to assist in this critical phase of cyber discovery.

Footprinting, at its core, is the process of collecting data about a target, whether it's an organization, network, or individual.

Imagine it as the detective work in the cybersecurity world, where the investigator seeks to uncover clues that might reveal vulnerabilities, weaknesses, or potential entry points.

One of the fundamental techniques in footprinting is passive information gathering, which involves collecting publicly available data without directly interacting with the target.

This method relies on the vast amount of information that individuals and organizations inadvertently expose through their online presence.

Passive footprinting often begins with a visit to search engines like Google.

These search engines serve as portals to the wealth of information available on the internet, and skilled footprinters know how to use them effectively.

By crafting specific search queries, an adept footprinting specialist can unearth hidden gems of data, discovering everything from domain names and subdomains to employee names and email addresses.

Beyond search engines, social media platforms are a goldmine of information.

People often share personal and professional details on platforms like Facebook, LinkedIn, and Twitter, providing a rich source of data for footprinters.

Pictures, posts, and connections can reveal organizational affiliations, relationships, and even the technology stack a company employs.

Online forums and discussion boards are another playground for footprinters.

These communities often contain discussions about technologies, vulnerabilities, and specific industry-related topics.

By monitoring these forums, a footprinter can gain insights into the technologies an organization uses and any ongoing issues or concerns.

Domain Name System (DNS) is a fundamental component of the internet, and it plays a significant role in footprinting.

DNS information, such as domain names, IP addresses, and mail server records, can be accessed through various online tools and databases.

By scrutinizing DNS records, a footprinter can build a more comprehensive picture of the target's digital infrastructure.

WHOIS databases provide registration information for domain names.

By querying these databases, footprinters can discover the names, addresses, and contact details of domain owners, which can be valuable in identifying key individuals or organizations of interest.

Reverse WHOIS lookup tools take this a step further, allowing footprinters to search for domain names associated with specific individuals or entities.

When it comes to active footprinting, the process involves directly interacting with the target's systems or networks.

This approach requires a higher level of caution, as it may trigger security alerts or expose the footprinter's activities.

Port scanning is a classic example of active footprinting.

It involves sending packets to a target's network to discover open ports and services.

This information can be used to assess the potential attack surface of the target.

Network mapping goes hand in hand with port scanning.

It aims to create a visual representation of the target's network infrastructure, showcasing the relationships between devices, servers, and routers.

By understanding the network's layout, a footprinter can identify potential points of entry or areas where vulnerabilities may exist.

While active footprinting techniques can be powerful, they must be executed with care and adherence to ethical and legal considerations.

Unauthorized access attempts or intrusive scanning can cross legal boundaries and may result in legal consequences.

Footprinting tools play a crucial role in streamlining the process and automating various aspects of reconnaissance.

For passive information gathering, tools like Maltego and theHarvester are popular choices among footprinters.

Maltego, for instance, provides a graphical interface for visualizing relationships between entities like domain names, email addresses, and social media profiles.

It allows users to aggregate data from various sources and create detailed graphs that aid in the reconnaissance process.

theHarvester, on the other hand, specializes in email address and subdomain enumeration, helping footprinters gather valuable contact information.

For active footprinting, tools like Nmap (Network Mapper) and Wireshark are indispensable.

Nmap is a versatile port scanning tool that can be used to discover open ports and services on target systems.

It also provides valuable information about the operating systems running on those systems.

Wireshark, on the other hand, is a packet analysis tool that allows footprinters to capture and analyze network traffic.

It can reveal vulnerabilities, weak authentication mechanisms, and other critical information.

As the world of cybersecurity continues to evolve, so do footprinting methods and tools.

Security professionals and ethical hackers are continually innovating and adapting to new technologies and threats.

The realm of mobile and cloud computing has introduced new challenges and opportunities for footprinting.

Mobile footprinting involves gathering information about mobile applications, their vulnerabilities, and the data they transmit.

Cloud footprinting focuses on assessing the security of cloud-based services, identifying potential misconfigurations or weaknesses in cloud deployments.

Machine learning and artificial intelligence are also playing a growing role in footprinting.

These technologies can help automate the analysis of vast amounts of data, enabling faster and more accurate reconnaissance.

In summary, footprinting is a dynamic and essential phase in the world of cybersecurity.

It serves as the foundation for understanding potential vulnerabilities and threats, enabling organizations and individuals to fortify their defenses.

The tools and methods employed in footprinting continue to evolve, reflecting the ever-changing landscape of digital security.

Whether you're a cybersecurity professional, an ethical hacker, or someone interested in safeguarding your digital presence, a deep understanding of footprinting methods and tools is key to navigating the complex terrain of modern cybersecurity.

Exploring real-world footprinting case studies provides a tangible perspective on the application of reconnaissance techniques in the field of cybersecurity.

These case studies illuminate how footprinting, often the first step in cyberattacks, plays a crucial role in understanding vulnerabilities and risks.

Consider a hypothetical scenario where an ethical hacker, tasked with testing the security of a financial institution, embarks on a reconnaissance mission.

The hacker begins with passive information gathering, scouring the internet for publicly available data about the bank.

Using open-source intelligence (OSINT) tools like Maltego and theHarvester, the hacker identifies the bank's website, email addresses associated with its domain, and social media profiles of key personnel.

While this information may seem innocuous, it forms the foundation for subsequent steps in the assessment.

Next, the hacker decides to perform active footprinting to gain a deeper understanding of the bank's digital infrastructure.

Using Nmap, a renowned port scanning tool, the hacker discovers that several ports on the bank's web server are open.

Digging further, the hacker uses Wireshark to analyze network traffic during the interaction with the bank's website.

This reveals potential vulnerabilities, such as weak encryption protocols and unauthenticated access to certain resources.

The hacker also employs a DNS enumeration tool to gather information about the bank's subdomains.

This information could be leveraged to target specific departments or services within the organization.

In another case, let's explore the footprinting activities of a cybersecurity consultant hired by a retail company.

The consultant's task is to identify potential security weaknesses in the company's e-commerce platform.

To begin, the consultant conducts passive footprinting by searching for information about the company online.

Using search engines, the consultant finds the company's website, social media profiles, and mentions in industry forums.

Additionally, the consultant discovers that the company's e-commerce platform is built on a specific content management system (CMS).

This information provides valuable insights into potential vulnerabilities associated with that CMS.

Moving to active footprinting, the consultant uses Nmap to scan the e-commerce server for open ports and services.

The scan reveals open ports that could be targeted for further analysis.

The consultant decides to employ a vulnerability scanning tool like Nessus to identify specific vulnerabilities in the e-commerce platform.

Nessus scans the system and reports several critical vulnerabilities related to outdated software and misconfigurations.

These vulnerabilities pose a significant risk to the security of the e-commerce platform and the sensitive customer data it handles.

In both of these cases, the reconnaissance activities played a pivotal role in identifying potential security risks and vulnerabilities.

However, it's important to emphasize that these cases involve ethical hacking and security assessments conducted with the explicit consent of the organizations involved.

Ethical hackers follow a strict code of conduct, ensuring that their activities are legal, authorized, and aligned with the organization's security goals.

Now, let's explore a more complex real-world example involving a multinational corporation with a diverse digital footprint.

This corporation operates in various sectors, including finance, healthcare, and energy, making it a prime target for cyberattacks.

The corporation's cybersecurity team regularly conducts footprinting to assess the security of its extensive network.

In this case, passive footprinting is ongoing, with the team continuously monitoring internet chatter, hacker forums, and social media for mentions of the corporation or potential threats.

They use specialized OSINT tools designed for enterprise-level intelligence gathering to sift through the vast amount of data available online.

Active footprinting is conducted periodically but cautiously, to avoid disrupting critical operations. The team employs Nmap, Wireshark, and other scanning tools to assess the security of critical systems and networks.

In addition to technical reconnaissance, the corporation's cybersecurity team conducts regular physical reconnaissance to evaluate the security of its physical locations, data centers, and offices.

This includes assessing access controls, surveillance systems, and environmental security measures.

The team also engages in social engineering tests to gauge the effectiveness of employee awareness training and to identify potential weaknesses in human-centric security measures.

One of the significant challenges in this case is the diversity of systems, networks, and technologies within the corporation's infrastructure.

The cybersecurity team must adapt their footprinting techniques to suit the unique characteristics of each sector while ensuring compliance with industry-specific regulations.

In summary, real-world footprinting case studies showcase the practical application of reconnaissance techniques in the cybersecurity landscape.

From ethical hackers uncovering vulnerabilities in e-commerce platforms to multinational corporations safeguarding their digital assets, the importance of reconnaissance cannot be overstated.

These examples underscore the critical role that footprinting plays in understanding and mitigating security risks in an increasingly interconnected and digital world.

Ultimately, the knowledge and insights gained through reconnaissance activities empower organizations and individuals to fortify their defenses and protect against cyber threats.

Chapter 3: Passive Information Gathering

Passive reconnaissance techniques represent the initial steps in gathering information about a target, be it an organization, network, or individual, without direct interaction or engagement.

In the world of cybersecurity, passive reconnaissance serves as a foundation upon which subsequent assessments and actions are built.

These techniques are akin to gathering breadcrumbs along a trail, breadcrumbs that, when meticulously collected and analyzed, reveal valuable insights about the target.

The primary goal of passive reconnaissance is to collect publicly available information, information that has been shared or exposed by the target either voluntarily or inadvertently.

Search engines, such as Google, are often the starting point for passive reconnaissance. They act as a gateway to the vast expanse of information available on the internet.

By crafting specific search queries, a cybersecurity professional can uncover domain names, subdomains, IP addresses, email addresses, and other potentially sensitive data.

Moreover, search engines can reveal files, directories, and documents inadvertently made public through misconfigured web servers or file-sharing services.

Social media platforms are another goldmine for passive reconnaissance. People and organizations frequently share personal and professional details on platforms like Facebook, LinkedIn, and Twitter.

Profiles, posts, and connections provide a rich source of information about individuals, their affiliations, roles, and even the technologies they use.

Online forums and discussion boards are yet another treasure trove of data. Communities often discuss technologies, vulnerabilities, and industry-specific topics.

Monitoring these forums allows cybersecurity professionals to gain insights into the technologies an organization employs, ongoing issues, or concerns related to security.

Passive reconnaissance also extends to DNS, the Domain Name System, which plays a pivotal role in internet infrastructure.

DNS information, such as domain names, IP addresses, mail server records, and more, can be accessed through various online tools and databases.

Scrutinizing DNS records allows cybersecurity professionals to build a more comprehensive understanding of a target's digital infrastructure.

WHOIS databases offer valuable insights into domain registration details. These databases contain information about the owner, registration date, and contact details of domain names.

Reverse WHOIS lookup tools take this a step further. They enable professionals to search for domain names associated with specific individuals or entities.

Passive reconnaissance is, in essence, about collecting information that is readily available, information that anyone can access without engaging in intrusive or potentially illegal activities.

This information forms the basis for informed decisions and further assessments.

Yet, passive reconnaissance does have its limitations. Its reliance on publicly available data means it may not uncover highly sensitive or confidential information.

Additionally, the information gathered may be outdated, as the digital landscape is constantly evolving.

Furthermore, passive reconnaissance is, by its nature, non-intrusive. It does not involve actively probing a target's systems or networks, which can limit its depth.

Despite these limitations, passive reconnaissance remains a critical and ethical practice in the realm of cybersecurity.

Its value lies in its non-disruptive, non-intrusive approach, which respects legal and ethical boundaries.

Cybersecurity professionals and ethical hackers leverage passive reconnaissance to establish a baseline understanding of a target.

This understanding allows for more precise and targeted assessments in subsequent phases of cybersecurity, such as vulnerability scanning and penetration testing.

In summary, passive reconnaissance techniques serve as the digital equivalent of a detective's investigation, where digital breadcrumbs lead to the discovery of valuable information about a target.

From search engine queries to social media exploration and DNS record scrutiny, these techniques form the initial steps in understanding the digital landscape of a target.

While passive reconnaissance has its limitations, it remains an essential and ethical practice in the cybersecurity arsenal, enabling professionals to gather insights, identify potential vulnerabilities, and make informed decisions in the ever-evolving digital landscape.

Exploring the art of leveraging publicly available information is like delving into a treasure trove of knowledge hidden in plain sight, waiting to be uncovered.

In the realm of cybersecurity, this skill is instrumental in understanding potential targets, identifying vulnerabilities, and shaping effective defense strategies.

Publicly available information, also known as open-source intelligence (OSINT), is a goldmine of data that individuals and organizations inadvertently expose through their online presence.

Imagine OSINT as the digital footprint of an entity—a footprint that, when properly examined, can reveal valuable insights.

At its core, leveraging publicly available information is the process of collecting data about a target, whether it's an organization, an individual, or an event, by tapping into openly accessible sources.

These sources can be as diverse as search engines, social media platforms, public records, websites, forums, and more.

The value of OSINT lies in its non-intrusive nature. It doesn't involve direct interaction with the target or invasive activities; rather, it relies on data willingly shared or made public.

Search engines, such as Google, are often the starting point for OSINT practitioners. They serve as gateways to the vast sea of information available on the internet.

By crafting specific search queries, one can uncover a plethora of details, including domain names, subdomains, IP addresses, email addresses, and much more.

Search engines can also reveal hidden gems like files, directories, and documents that may have been inadvertently exposed on the web.

Social media platforms are treasure troves of personal and professional information. Individuals and organizations often share intimate details about themselves and their activities.

Profiles, posts, connections, and interactions—all of these provide a rich source of data. They shed light on people's interests, affiliations, job roles, and even the technologies they use.

For instance, a cybersecurity practitioner can analyze an organization's LinkedIn page to gain insights into its workforce, including key personnel and their professional backgrounds.

Online forums and discussion boards are digital watering holes where people convene to discuss a wide array of topics, including technology and security.

Monitoring these forums can offer valuable insights into an organization's technological preferences, ongoing challenges, and even potential security vulnerabilities.

The knowledge gleaned from these discussions can be instrumental in understanding a target's technological landscape.

Publicly accessible DNS information is another facet of OSINT. The Domain Name System plays a pivotal role in the functioning of the internet.

DNS information, including domain names, IP addresses, mail server records, and more, can be accessed through various online tools and databases.

Scrutinizing DNS records provides a deeper understanding of a target's digital infrastructure. It unveils the relationships between domains, servers, and services.

WHOIS databases offer additional insights. They contain registration details about domain names, including ownership, registration date, and contact information.

Reverse WHOIS lookup tools take this a step further. They allow OSINT practitioners to search for domain names associated with specific individuals or organizations.

Email addresses, often shared publicly on websites, forums, and social media, can be another valuable source of information. They can lead to additional insights about an individual's or organization's online presence.

In essence, leveraging publicly available information is a subtle yet powerful art that forms the foundation for informed decisions and effective cybersecurity strategies.

It's important to note that OSINT doesn't stop at technology-related data; it extends to various domains, including geopolitics, finance, and even human behavior.

For example, OSINT can be employed to monitor global events, analyze social sentiment, or track emerging trends in various industries.

The applications of OSINT are diverse and extend beyond the cybersecurity realm. It has become an indispensable tool for journalists, researchers, law enforcement agencies, and many others.

However, OSINT comes with its own set of challenges and ethical considerations. While the information gathered is publicly available, it should always be collected and used responsibly and legally.

Respecting individuals' privacy and adhering to applicable laws and regulations is paramount.

Moreover, OSINT practitioners must be mindful of the potential for misinformation or manipulated data on the internet. Verifying the authenticity of sources is a crucial part of the process.

As technology continues to advance and the digital landscape evolves, OSINT techniques and tools also adapt and expand.

Machine learning and artificial intelligence are increasingly employed to sift through vast amounts of data, allowing for more efficient and accurate analysis.

In summary, the art of leveraging publicly available information is a skill that empowers individuals and organizations to navigate the vast digital landscape effectively.

Whether in the realm of cybersecurity, investigative journalism, or research, OSINT plays a pivotal role in uncovering valuable insights and shaping informed decisions.

It's a reminder that in our interconnected world, a wealth of knowledge is at our fingertips, waiting to be discovered by those who know where to look.

Chapter 4: Active Information Gathering

Exploring the realm of active reconnaissance tools and tactics is akin to embarking on a digital journey, where the aim is to gather information about a target through direct interaction and probing.

Active reconnaissance represents a proactive approach in the realm of cybersecurity, where the objective is to identify potential vulnerabilities and weaknesses that could be exploited.

This phase involves more than just observing; it entails actively scanning, probing, and interacting with the target to gain a deeper understanding of its digital infrastructure.

One of the fundamental tactics in active reconnaissance is port scanning, a technique used to identify open ports and services on a target system or network.

Port scanning tools, such as Nmap, are commonly employed for this purpose. They send packets to a target's IP address, probing for open ports and available services.

By identifying open ports, a cybersecurity practitioner can gain insights into the attack surface of the target and the potential entry points that exist.

Service enumeration is another critical aspect of active reconnaissance. Once open ports are identified, the next step is to determine the specific services running on those ports.

This information helps in understanding the technologies and applications in use, which can be instrumental in identifying potential vulnerabilities.

Banner grabbing is a technique used to extract information about the target's services. It involves capturing and analyzing the banners or headers provided by services upon connection.

These banners often reveal details such as the service name, version, and sometimes even configuration information, which can be valuable for subsequent assessments.

Vulnerability scanning is a crucial tactic in active reconnaissance. Vulnerability scanning tools, like Nessus and OpenVAS, are used to identify potential security weaknesses in a target's systems and applications.

These tools systematically scan the target's network and services, checking for known vulnerabilities and misconfigurations.

The results of vulnerability scans provide a prioritized list of potential issues that can be addressed to improve security.

Operating system fingerprinting is another tactic employed in active reconnaissance. This involves identifying the specific operating system running on a target system.

By analyzing network responses and behavior, fingerprinting tools like OSFingerprint can deduce the underlying operating system with a high degree of accuracy.

Network mapping and enumeration are essential components of active reconnaissance. Network mapping aims to create a visual representation of the target's network infrastructure.

It showcases the relationships between devices, servers, routers, and other network components.

By understanding the network layout, a practitioner can identify potential points of entry and areas where vulnerabilities may exist.

Enumeration, on the other hand, involves extracting information about network resources, such as user accounts, shares, and services.

Enumeration tools like Enum4linux and SMBclient are commonly used to gather valuable insights into the target's resources and user accounts.

Active reconnaissance tactics also extend to web applications, where practitioners use web application scanning tools like Burp Suite and OWASP ZAP.

These tools help identify vulnerabilities in web applications, such as SQL injection, cross-site scripting (XSS), and authentication weaknesses.

Automated web scanners crawl through web pages, interact with forms, and analyze responses to discover potential vulnerabilities.

Brute force attacks represent another facet of active reconnaissance. These attacks involve systematically trying a large number of possible passwords or combinations to gain unauthorized access.

Brute force tools, such as Hydra and John the Ripper, automate these attempts, making it feasible to crack weak passwords.

Credential harvesting and password spraying are variants of brute force attacks, focusing on collecting valid usernames and passwords.

Social engineering plays a role in active reconnaissance as well. While not purely technical, it leverages human psychology to gather information or gain unauthorized access.

Techniques like phishing, pretexting, and tailgating manipulate trust and curiosity to extract sensitive data or access restricted areas.

In addition to technical tactics, active reconnaissance can involve physical reconnaissance, where an attacker or assessor physically assesses an organization's security measures.

This can include physically visiting an office or data center to assess access controls, surveillance systems, and environmental security measures.

The use of drones for aerial reconnaissance is also an emerging trend, allowing for physical assessment from the air.

As with all cybersecurity practices, ethical and legal considerations are paramount in active reconnaissance. Unauthorized access attempts, intrusive scanning, or invasive techniques can cross legal boundaries and lead to severe consequences.

It's essential to conduct active reconnaissance activities with explicit consent and within the framework of ethical guidelines.

In summary, active reconnaissance tools and tactics represent a proactive approach to understanding and assessing a target's digital and physical security posture.

From port scanning and vulnerability assessment to web application scanning and social engineering, these tactics form a critical phase in the broader landscape of cybersecurity.

When employed responsibly and ethically, active reconnaissance provides valuable insights that empower organizations to address vulnerabilities, strengthen their defenses, and safeguard their digital assets.

Mitigating risks in active information gathering is an essential aspect of ethical and responsible cybersecurity practices.

As we've explored, active reconnaissance techniques involve probing and interacting with target systems and networks, making them inherently more intrusive than passive reconnaissance.

While active information gathering is a valuable part of the cybersecurity toolkit, it comes with its own set of challenges and potential pitfalls that must be carefully managed.

One of the primary risks in active information gathering is the potential for disruption or unintended consequences.

Probing a target's systems or network can trigger alarms, alerts, or even lead to performance degradation or system downtime.

To mitigate this risk, cybersecurity professionals must always seek explicit consent from the organization or individual being assessed.

Ethical hacking and penetration testing should always follow strict rules of engagement to ensure that assessments are conducted in a controlled and responsible manner.

Another risk in active information gathering is the possibility of legal and regulatory violations.

Unauthorized access attempts, intrusive scans, or other aggressive tactics can cross legal boundaries and result in legal consequences.

It's crucial to operate within the confines of the law and adhere to relevant regulations when conducting active reconnaissance.

Ethical hackers and cybersecurity practitioners must be well-versed in the legal aspects of their work and obtain the necessary permissions and approvals.

False positives and inaccurate findings represent a challenge in active information gathering.

Vulnerability scanning tools and other active reconnaissance techniques may generate false alarms or inaccurately report vulnerabilities.

To address this risk, cybersecurity professionals should verify and validate their findings to avoid unnecessary panic or disruption.

Furthermore, misinterpretation of results can occur when conducting active reconnaissance.

Without a deep understanding of the target's environment, it's possible to misjudge the severity of vulnerabilities or misattribute findings to the wrong systems or applications.

To mitigate this risk, cybersecurity practitioners should engage in thorough analysis and cross-reference findings with contextual information.

Cybersecurity professionals must also be mindful of the potential for exposure during active reconnaissance.

Intrusive activities can leave traces or fingerprints that attackers might exploit if they gain access to the reconnaissance tools or methods used.

To protect against this risk, practitioners should secure their reconnaissance tools, limit access to sensitive information, and employ encryption and secure communication channels.

Collateral damage is another risk in active information gathering.

Inadvertently affecting systems or networks not directly related to the target can occur, potentially causing disruption or damage.

To prevent collateral damage, active reconnaissance activities should be tightly scoped and focused on the intended target.

It's also crucial to maintain thorough documentation of the reconnaissance process.

This documentation serves multiple purposes: it provides a record of activities for auditing and compliance purposes, assists in validating findings, and helps in communicating results to stakeholders.

Moreover, documentation can be invaluable in incident response and remediation efforts should vulnerabilities be discovered.

In the realm of web application scanning, a specific risk involves unintentionally triggering security mechanisms, such as intrusion detection systems or rate limiting.

To mitigate this risk, practitioners can adjust the scanning speed and employ techniques to evade detection, such as randomizing scan intervals.

As active reconnaissance tactics continue to evolve, so do the countermeasures employed by organizations to protect their digital assets.

Target organizations may implement security measures to detect and thwart reconnaissance attempts.

This includes intrusion detection and prevention systems (IDPS), web application firewalls (WAFs), and advanced monitoring tools.

To mitigate the risk of detection and interference, cybersecurity practitioners may employ techniques like stealth scanning and traffic obfuscation.

In summary, mitigating risks in active information gathering is a critical part of ethical cybersecurity practices.

While active reconnaissance techniques offer valuable insights, they must be conducted responsibly, within legal boundaries, and with explicit consent.

Cybersecurity professionals must also be vigilant about the potential for disruption, legal violations, false positives, and exposure during their activities.

Thorough documentation, careful scoping, and adaptability in response to evolving security measures are key strategies to mitigate these risks effectively.

Ultimately, the responsible use of active information gathering techniques is essential in maintaining the balance between identifying vulnerabilities and safeguarding the integrity and availability of systems and networks.

Chapter 5: Open Source Intelligence (OSINT)

Harnessing the power of Open Source Intelligence, or OSINT, is like opening a window to a world of information that's hiding in plain sight on the internet.

OSINT is a valuable and versatile tool in the field of cybersecurity and intelligence, allowing individuals and organizations to gather insights from publicly available sources.

At its core, OSINT is about collecting data from open sources, sources that are accessible to anyone with an internet connection.

These sources include websites, social media platforms, forums, news articles, public records, and more.

OSINT practitioners use a variety of techniques and tools to sift through this vast sea of information and extract valuable insights.

Search engines, like Google, are a fundamental starting point for OSINT. They serve as gateways to the wealth of data available on the internet.

By crafting specific search queries, OSINT analysts can uncover a treasure trove of information, including domain names, IP addresses, email addresses, and more.

The art of crafting precise search queries is a skill that OSINT practitioners hone over time, allowing them to uncover hidden gems of information.

Social media platforms are another goldmine for OSINT. People and organizations often share personal and professional details on platforms like Facebook, Twitter, LinkedIn, and Instagram.

Profiles, posts, connections, and interactions provide rich data about individuals, their interests, affiliations, and activities.

For example, OSINT analysts can use LinkedIn to identify key personnel in an organization, learn about their roles, and even identify potential targets for spear-phishing attacks.

Online forums and discussion boards are digital communities where people gather to discuss a wide range of topics, including technology, security, and industry-specific subjects. These forums often contain discussions about technologies, vulnerabilities, and current trends.

OSINT analysts can monitor these forums to gain insights into the latest developments in various fields, including cybersecurity.

Public records, such as court documents, property records, business registrations, and government websites, are valuable sources of information.

These records can reveal details about individuals, businesses, and organizations, including legal issues, financial data, and ownership information.

Government websites, in particular, are excellent sources for data related to licenses, permits, regulations, and public expenditures.

Web scraping and data mining tools are often employed to automate the collection of data from websites and online sources.

These tools can help OSINT analysts extract large volumes of information efficiently.

One of the key advantages of OSINT is its non-intrusive nature. OSINT relies on data that is willingly shared or publicly accessible.

There is no need for hacking, intrusive scanning, or unauthorized access.

However, the power of OSINT lies not only in the sources but also in the analysis. OSINT practitioners excel at analyzing and correlating data from multiple sources.

For example, they can use email addresses found on a public forum to identify social media profiles and further expand their understanding of an individual's online presence.

Another crucial aspect of OSINT is the ability to verify information. The internet is rife with misinformation and fake data.

OSINT analysts must employ critical thinking and fact-checking to ensure the accuracy of the information they gather.

OSINT is not limited to cybersecurity; it has applications in various domains. Journalists use OSINT to research stories, track down sources, and verify facts.

Law enforcement agencies employ OSINT to aid investigations and gather information about suspects or criminal activities.

Businesses can use OSINT for competitive analysis, market research, and reputation management.

OSINT also plays a vital role in geopolitical analysis, allowing researchers to monitor events, track the activities of state actors, and assess international developments.

Despite its numerous advantages, OSINT does come with its own set of challenges. One of the primary challenges is the volume of data available.

The internet is vast, and sifting through mountains of information can be overwhelming.

OSINT analysts must develop effective search strategies and tools to streamline the process.

Another challenge is the ethical and legal considerations surrounding OSINT. While the information gathered is publicly accessible, there are limits to what can be done with it.

OSINT practitioners must respect privacy, adhere to laws and regulations, and obtain the necessary permissions when required.

Additionally, OSINT analysts must be cautious about the potential for misinformation or manipulated data.

The internet is a breeding ground for fake news, doctored images, and misinformation campaigns.

As such, OSINT practitioners must employ critical thinking, fact-checking, and source verification to ensure the accuracy of their findings.

In summary, harnessing the power of OSINT is a valuable skill in the digital age.

It allows individuals and organizations to gather insights, make informed decisions, and stay ahead of emerging trends and threats.

The art of OSINT involves not only collecting data from publicly available sources but also analyzing, verifying, and correlating that data to create a comprehensive picture.

As technology continues to advance and the digital landscape evolves, OSINT remains a powerful tool for those who know how to use it effectively, opening windows to a world of information hidden in plain sight.

Diving deeper into the world of Open Source Intelligence (OSINT), we uncover a realm of advanced techniques and resources that elevate the practice to new heights.

Advanced OSINT techniques go beyond basic searches and extend into more sophisticated methods of information gathering.

They empower OSINT practitioners to unearth hidden insights, track elusive targets, and paint a more complete picture of their subjects.

One of the advanced OSINT techniques involves the use of specialized search engines.

While Google is a powerful tool, there are search engines tailored specifically for OSINT, such as Shodan and Censys, which focus on scanning and indexing internet-connected devices and services.

These specialized search engines allow practitioners to discover vulnerable devices, exposed databases, and other potentially sensitive information.

Another advanced OSINT technique is the use of social media analysis tools.

These tools, such as Maltego and SpiderFoot, automate the process of gathering and correlating data from social media platforms.

They can reveal relationships, connections, and patterns that might be difficult to discern through manual searches.

Geo-location techniques are valuable in advanced OSINT.

By analyzing geotagged data from photos, social media posts, or other sources, practitioners can pinpoint the physical locations of individuals or objects.

This information can be crucial in various contexts, from tracking criminals to identifying the locations of protests or events.

Advanced OSINT practitioners often leverage domain and email analysis.

They delve deep into the online infrastructure of a target by examining domain name registration records, WHOIS data, and MX records for email.

This helps in identifying the entities behind websites, assessing the legitimacy of email sources, and mapping out an organization's digital footprint.

OSINT analysts also make use of advanced data visualization techniques.

Tools like Gephi and Tableau enable practitioners to transform raw data into interactive and insightful visualizations.

These visualizations can reveal connections, trends, and anomalies that might not be immediately apparent in raw data.

Moreover, reverse image search is an advanced OSINT technique that has gained prominence.

By uploading an image to search engines like Google Images or TinEye, analysts can discover where else on the internet that image has appeared.

This can be valuable for tracking the spread of misinformation, identifying original sources of images, or locating similar images associated with a subject.

Advanced OSINT extends into the realm of linguistic analysis.

Language identification and sentiment analysis tools can help in understanding the tone, language, and sentiments expressed in textual data.

This can be particularly useful for tracking sentiment trends on social media or identifying the languages spoken by a target.

In the world of advanced OSINT, dark web investigations play a crucial role.

The dark web is a hidden part of the internet where anonymity and secrecy prevail.

Advanced OSINT practitioners may use specialized tools and techniques to access and monitor dark web forums, marketplaces, and communities.

They gather intelligence on illegal activities, cyber threats, and emerging trends in the hidden corners of the web.

The use of advanced OSINT resources is equally important.

Subscription-based services like Recorded Future and Echosec offer access to extensive databases of real-time and historical data.

These resources provide OSINT practitioners with a wealth of information, from threat intelligence to news mentions and social media data.

Web scraping, while not new, continues to be a powerful tool in advanced OSINT.

It involves extracting data from websites and online sources using automated scripts.

Web scraping allows analysts to collect large volumes of data quickly, which can then be analyzed for patterns or anomalies.

Additionally, the use of APIs (Application Programming Interfaces) is a common practice in advanced OSINT.

Many websites and online platforms provide APIs that allow for programmatic access to their data.

OSINT practitioners can leverage APIs to retrieve data from sources like Twitter, Facebook, or news websites, enabling more efficient and real-time data collection.

While advanced OSINT techniques and resources expand the horizons of information gathering, they also come with their own set of challenges and ethical considerations.

Respecting privacy, adhering to legal boundaries, and ensuring data accuracy remain paramount.

Moreover, advanced OSINT requires a continuous commitment to learning and staying updated with evolving technologies and techniques.

In summary, advanced OSINT techniques and resources are essential tools in the arsenal of modern information gatherers.

They empower practitioners to uncover hidden insights, track elusive subjects, and navigate the ever-changing landscape of the digital world.

From specialized search engines to linguistic analysis and dark web investigations, advanced OSINT opens new avenues for understanding the complex web of online information.

Chapter 6: Using Search Engines Effectively

Let's delve into the fascinating world of search engine operators and filters, powerful tools that can enhance your online research and information gathering.

Search engines, like Google, are indispensable in our quest for information on the vast internet.

But did you know that you can significantly refine your search results and uncover hidden gems using specific commands and filters?

One of the most basic yet effective search operators is the use of quotation marks.

When you enclose a phrase in double quotation marks, the search engine will look for the exact phrase, rather than individual words scattered across a page.

For example, searching for "climate change effects" will return results that specifically mention this phrase.

Boolean operators, such as AND, OR, and NOT, allow you to create more complex queries.

Using AND narrows your search by requiring both terms to be present in the results.

For instance, "cybersecurity AND data breaches" will find pages that contain both terms.

On the other hand, OR broadens your search by finding pages that contain either of the terms.

For instance, "smartphones OR tablets" will return results related to either smartphones or tablets.

NOT helps you exclude specific terms from your search.

For example, "apple NOT fruit" will return results related to the technology company rather than the fruit.

Another handy operator is the wildcard (*).

You can use an asterisk to represent a missing word or part of a word when you're unsure of the exact phrase.

For instance, "search * optimization" will find results related to search engine optimization, even if the middle word varies.

The site operator allows you to narrow your search to a specific website or domain.

By typing "site:" followed by a website's address, you can limit your search results to that particular site.

For instance, "site:wikipedia.org space exploration" will find information about space exploration only on Wikipedia.

The filetype operator is helpful when you're looking for specific types of files, such as PDFs or Word documents.

By using "filetype:" followed by the file extension, you can narrow your results to that file type.

For example, "filetype:pdf climate change report" will find PDF documents related to climate change reports.

The intitle and inurl operators allow you to search for specific words in the title or URL of a web page.

For instance, "intitle:cybersecurity tips" will return results with "cybersecurity" in the title.

Similarly, "inurl:recipes chocolate" will find URLs that contain "chocolate" in the address.

You can use the related operator to discover websites related to a specific domain.

For example, "related:wikipedia.org" will provide you with websites that are similar in content or context to Wikipedia.

The cache operator allows you to view the cached version of a web page as it appeared when the search engine last crawled it.

By using "cache:" followed by the URL, you can access a snapshot of the page.

Filters also play a crucial role in refining your search results. Most search engines offer various filters to help you find exactly what you're looking for.

You can filter results by date to see the most recent information.

This is particularly useful when you're searching for news, events, or updates.

Language filters allow you to specify the language of the results, ensuring that you get information in the language you prefer.

Search engines also provide location-based filters, which are handy for finding local businesses, services, or news.

If you're searching for images or videos, you can filter results based on media type.

This makes it easy to find visuals or multimedia content related to your query.

Relevance filters help you sort results by their perceived relevance to your query, putting the most relevant results at the top.

These filters are especially useful when you're dealing with a large number of results.

Safe search filters can be enabled to filter out explicit or adult content from your search results.

They provide a safer browsing experience, particularly for family-friendly searches.

Search engines also offer advanced search settings that allow you to fine-tune your results even further.

You can access these settings to customize your search experience according to your preferences.

Using these search operators and filters effectively can save you time and help you find precisely the information you're looking for.

Whether you're a student conducting research, a professional seeking specific data, or simply a curious explorer of the web, mastering these tools can enhance your online journey.

So, the next time you embark on a digital quest for knowledge, remember the power of search operators and filters at your fingertips, ready to assist you in uncovering the information you seek.

Exploring advanced search techniques is like unlocking the hidden potential of the digital world, enabling you to discover valuable information efficiently and effectively.

In the vast sea of data on the internet, refining your search skills can make a world of difference in finding the precise information you need.

Boolean operators, a fundamental tool in advanced searching, allow you to create complex queries by combining keywords with logical operators like AND, OR, and NOT.

For instance, you can use "AND" to narrow down your search results by requiring both keywords to appear in the results.

Using "OR" broadens your search by finding pages that contain either of the keywords, while "NOT" excludes specific terms from your results.

By mastering Boolean operators, you can tailor your searches to be as specific or broad as needed, ensuring that you find the information you're looking for.

Wildcards, another advanced search technique, empower you to search for variations of a word or phrase.

For instance, an asterisk (*) can represent one or more missing letters in a word.

This is particularly helpful when you're unsure of the exact spelling or when you want to find multiple forms of a word.

Using a question mark (?) can substitute for a single letter within a word, enabling you to find words with uncertain or variable letters.

Regular expressions, although more advanced, provide even greater flexibility in pattern-based searching.

They allow you to define specific patterns or sequences of characters to match in your search.

For example, you can use regular expressions to find phone numbers, email addresses, or specific data formats within documents.

Proximity searching is a technique that helps you find keywords or phrases that appear close to each other in a document.

By specifying a maximum distance or number of words between terms, you can pinpoint relevant information more accurately.

This is especially useful when you're conducting research and need to identify connections between concepts.

Search engines often provide advanced search operators like "intitle," "inurl," and "filetype" to refine your results further.

The "intitle" operator allows you to search for pages where specific keywords appear in the title.

For instance, "intitle:cybersecurity tips" will find pages with "cybersecurity" in the title.

The "inurl" operator helps you find pages with specific keywords in the URL.

For example, "inurl:recipes chocolate" will locate pages that contain "chocolate" in the web address.

The "filetype" operator is handy for finding specific types of files, such as PDFs or Word documents, by specifying the file extension.

Mastering these operators can save you time and help you locate content in the desired format.

Google's Advanced Search page offers an array of options to fine-tune your searches, including the ability to filter by language, region, file type, and more.

These settings provide a user-friendly interface for utilizing advanced search techniques without needing to memorize specific operators.

Moreover, you can use search engines to limit your results to specific timeframes.

For instance, you can filter results to show only those from the past week, month, or year.

This is invaluable when you're seeking the latest news or updates on a topic.

Learning to use search filters effectively can also enhance your information discovery.

You can filter results by type, such as images, videos, news, or books, to access content that matches your preferred format.

Location-based filters are useful for finding local businesses, services, or events in a specific area.

Whether you're planning a trip or looking for nearby restaurants, these filters can be invaluable.

Another advanced technique involves the use of "site:" followed by a specific website's domain to limit your search to that site.

This is particularly handy when you want to search within a specific website or domain.

"Related:" is another operator that helps you find websites related to a particular domain.

It can lead you to similar sources or alternative perspectives on a topic.

Search engines also allow you to explore image search with advanced options.

You can find visually similar images or search by color, size, or type to locate graphics or illustrations that suit your needs.

Filtering by usage rights ensures that you find images that are free to use for your specific purposes, whether for personal or commercial use.

Finally, you can delve into advanced settings in your search engine's preferences or settings menu.

Here, you can customize your search experience, including options like SafeSearch filters and personalized results.

This allows you to tailor your searches to match your preferences and requirements.

In summary, mastering advanced search techniques is a valuable skill in today's information-rich digital landscape.

These techniques empower you to navigate the vast sea of data more effectively, allowing you to pinpoint the information you need quickly.

Whether you're conducting research, planning a trip, or simply satisfying your curiosity, advanced searching opens doors to a world of knowledge waiting to be discovered at your fingertips.

Chapter 7: Social Engineering and Reconnaissance

Understanding the psychology of social engineering is like peeling back the layers of human behavior to reveal the subtle and intricate ways in which people can be manipulated.

Social engineering, in the realm of cybersecurity and beyond, relies on the art of deception and manipulation to influence individuals into taking certain actions or revealing confidential information.

At its core, social engineering exploits the vulnerabilities of the human mind, relying on psychological principles to achieve its goals.

One key psychological principle underpinning social engineering is the innate human tendency to trust.

People tend to trust others, especially when they appear credible, knowledgeable, or hold positions of authority.

Social engineers often leverage this trust by posing as trusted figures or using persuasive tactics to create a sense of trustworthiness.

For example, a hacker might impersonate a colleague, IT support personnel, or a customer service representative to gain access to sensitive information.

Another psychological concept at play in social engineering is reciprocity.

Humans have a natural inclination to reciprocate when someone does something for them.

Social engineers take advantage of this by offering assistance, gifts, or favors to their targets, creating a sense of indebtedness.

Once the target feels obligated, they may be more willing to comply with requests, even if they seem unusual or suspicious.

Authority is a potent psychological trigger exploited by social engineers.

People tend to follow orders or requests from those they perceive as authoritative figures.

Social engineers often adopt roles that convey authority, such as pretending to be a supervisor, manager, or law enforcement officer.

This perceived authority can compel targets to comply with requests they might otherwise question.

Scarcity is another psychological principle commonly exploited in social engineering.

People tend to desire things more when they perceive them as scarce or in high demand.

Social engineers create a sense of urgency or scarcity to manipulate targets into taking immediate action, bypassing critical thinking.

Fear is a powerful emotion that social engineers tap into to manipulate their targets.

By creating a sense of fear or impending danger, they can coerce individuals into disclosing sensitive information or performing actions they wouldn't under normal circumstances.

For instance, a social engineer might threaten legal action or claim that a target's account has been compromised to prompt immediate compliance.

Establishing rapport is crucial in social engineering.

Building a connection with the target helps create a sense of familiarity and trust.

Social engineers often engage in small talk, mirroring the target's behavior, or demonstrating shared interests to establish rapport quickly.

Reciprocity, authority, and scarcity are principles that can be employed to manipulate targets by creating a sense of obligation, trust, or urgency.

Fear and rapport, on the other hand, focus on evoking specific emotions to influence behavior.

In the world of social engineering, pretexting is a common technique used to fabricate a credible scenario or pretext to manipulate the target.

The social engineer constructs a believable story or situation to gain the target's trust and compliance.

For example, a pretexting scenario might involve a social engineer posing as an employee who needs urgent access to a restricted area, citing a fabricated work order.

Phishing, a prevalent form of social engineering, exploits email communication to deceive and manipulate recipients.

Phishing emails often appear legitimate, with convincing logos, sender addresses, and messages designed to lure recipients into clicking on malicious links or revealing sensitive information.

Phishing preys on individuals' trust in email communication and their curiosity or fear of missing out.

Tailgating, also known as "piggybacking," is a physical social engineering technique where an attacker gains unauthorized access to a secure area by following a legitimate employee.

By blending in and appearing non-threatening, the attacker relies on the target's politeness and reluctance to challenge strangers.

Social engineers use baiting to entice targets into taking certain actions.

They offer something attractive, such as a free download, a USB drive, or a link to a supposed interesting video.

Unbeknownst to the target, these baits may carry malware or lead to malicious websites.

The concept of "liking" plays a significant role in social engineering.

People are more likely to comply with requests from individuals they like or with whom they share common interests.

Social engineers exploit this by creating a likable persona or by impersonating someone the target knows and likes.

While the psychology of social engineering is instrumental in understanding its techniques, it's equally crucial to recognize and defend against such manipulation.

Education and awareness are fundamental in protecting against social engineering attacks.

Training individuals to recognize common tactics, red flags, and deceptive techniques can significantly reduce vulnerability.

Organizations should implement robust security policies and procedures, emphasizing the importance of verifying identities and being cautious about sharing sensitive information.

Technological safeguards, such as email filtering for phishing attempts, can provide an additional layer of protection.

Moreover, maintaining a healthy skepticism and a habit of verifying requests, especially those involving sensitive information or unusual circumstances, can thwart many social engineering attempts.

In summary, the psychology of social engineering is a fascinating and complex subject.

Understanding the psychological principles that underlie these manipulation techniques is essential in both recognizing and defending against them.

By combining awareness, education, and technological safeguards, individuals and organizations can better protect themselves against the deceptive tactics employed by social engineers in the digital age.

Delving into the world of cybersecurity, we come across a powerful and versatile tool known as the Social Engineering

Toolkit (SET), which opens the door to a range of exploitation methods that hackers employ to manipulate and deceive their targets.

The Social Engineering Toolkit is not a physical toolkit but rather a software framework designed to automate and streamline various social engineering attacks.

It serves as a potent resource for both ethical hackers and malicious actors, illustrating the dual nature of technology as a force for good and a tool for exploitation.

SET is an open-source tool that provides a menu-driven interface for launching a wide array of social engineering attacks with ease.

It simplifies the process of crafting convincing attack scenarios, allowing users to manipulate human behavior and exploit vulnerabilities in the human psyche.

One of the key features of the Social Engineering Toolkit is its ability to generate phishing emails, a common and highly effective form of social engineering attack.

Phishing emails are designed to appear legitimate and trustworthy, often mimicking official communications from trusted entities such as banks, social media platforms, or online services.

With SET, users can craft convincing phishing emails and deploy them on a targeted group of recipients, luring them into clicking on malicious links or providing sensitive information.

Another powerful feature of SET is the creation of malicious websites that mirror legitimate ones.

Known as "cloning" websites, these replicas are designed to trick visitors into thinking they are interacting with a legitimate service.

Users can craft convincing login pages, online forms, or download portals to capture credentials, personal information, or even malware installations.

Social engineers often leverage the sense of urgency or fear to manipulate their targets.

SET allows users to create scenarios where targets believe they are in immediate danger or face serious consequences, compelling them to take specific actions without questioning.

For example, an attacker might create a fake warning message about a security breach, urging users to click on a link to change their password urgently.

By exploiting human emotions, social engineers increase the likelihood of success.

Social engineers are well aware of the human tendency to trust authoritative figures or institutions.

SET enables users to impersonate trusted entities, such as IT support personnel, supervisors, or law enforcement, to gain the trust of their targets.

This authority can be used to elicit sensitive information, request immediate action, or create a false sense of security.

Reciprocity is a psychological principle that social engineers often manipulate.

SET allows attackers to offer apparent benefits or rewards, fostering a sense of indebtedness in their targets.

For instance, an attacker might promise free software downloads or access to exclusive content in exchange for personal information.

The target, feeling obligated, may be more willing to comply with the request.

SET provides tools to create enticing bait scenarios that exploit human curiosity.

Users can craft scenarios involving enticing offers, contests, or downloads to lure targets into clicking on malicious links or downloading malware.

These baiting techniques capitalize on the desire for something valuable or intriguing, driving targets to take action without careful consideration.

In many social engineering attacks, establishing rapport is crucial.

SET allows users to engage in automated conversation scenarios, mimicking friendly interactions to build trust and familiarity with the target.

By mirroring the target's behavior or demonstrating shared interests, social engineers can create a false sense of connection, making it easier to manipulate the target.

The psychology of scarcity is harnessed through SET by creating scenarios where targets believe they have a limited opportunity to act.

For example, attackers can craft messages claiming that a time-limited offer or a limited number of spots are available, pressuring targets to respond quickly without hesitation.

Despite the power and capabilities of the Social Engineering Toolkit, it's essential to remember that it has legitimate uses as well.

Ethical hackers and cybersecurity professionals employ SET to assess and improve an organization's security posture.

By conducting controlled social engineering tests, they can identify vulnerabilities and educate employees about the risks of falling victim to such attacks.

However, the misuse of SET for malicious purposes is a serious concern.

To defend against social engineering attacks, individuals and organizations should invest in cybersecurity training and awareness programs.

Employees should be educated about the various forms of social engineering, red flags to watch for, and the importance of verifying requests, especially those involving sensitive information.

Implementing strong email filtering and security policies can help detect and block phishing attempts.

Furthermore, multi-factor authentication (MFA) should be encouraged to add an extra layer of security, making it more difficult for attackers to compromise accounts.

In summary, the Social Engineering Toolkit is a potent tool that underscores the need for heightened cybersecurity awareness and vigilance.

Understanding the exploitation methods it facilitates allows individuals and organizations to better defend against social engineering attacks.

By recognizing the psychological tactics used by attackers, we can bolster our defenses and mitigate the risks associated with social engineering in the digital age.

Chapter 8: Network Scanning and Enumeration

Let's embark on a journey into the realm of cybersecurity, where we'll explore the fascinating world of port scanning and banner grabbing—two essential techniques used to probe and understand the security posture of networked systems.

Port scanning, at its core, is a method used to identify open ports on a target system.

A port, in this context, refers to a specific communication endpoint that allows data to flow in and out of a computer.

Think of ports as doors to a building; some are wide open for anyone to enter, while others remain securely locked.

Why is knowing which doors are open important? Well, in the world of cybersecurity, open ports can be potential entry points for attackers.

Understanding which doors are ajar allows security professionals to strengthen their defenses.

Port scanning is akin to knocking on all the doors of a building to see which ones yield a response.

The scanning process involves sending network packets to a range of ports on a target system and observing how the system responds.

The responses received (or lack thereof) provide valuable information about the state of each port.

The simplest form of port scanning is the "connect" scan, also known as a full-open scan.

In this scan, the scanner attempts to establish a full connection with each port, just like a visitor knocking on a door and waiting for someone to answer.

If a connection is successfully established, it means the port is open and actively accepting incoming connections.

However, connect scanning can be easily detected by security systems, as it generates a complete handshake with the target, leaving a trail.

A more stealthy approach is the "SYN" scan, also known as a half-open or stealth scan.

In this method, the scanner sends a SYN packet to the target port and waits for a response.

If the port is open, it responds with a SYN-ACK packet, indicating that it's willing to establish a connection.

But instead of completing the handshake, the scanner sends a RST (reset) packet, closing the connection without fully establishing it.

This approach is less likely to trigger alarms on the target system, making it a popular choice for penetration testers and attackers.

UDP scanning is another variant of port scanning that targets the User Datagram Protocol (UDP), which is connectionless and less reliable than TCP.

UDP scans involve sending UDP packets to various ports and observing the responses.

If the target responds with an ICMP "Port Unreachable" message, it indicates that the port is closed.

However, if no response is received, it suggests that the port may be open or filtered by a firewall.

Now, let's shift our focus to banner grabbing, which complements port scanning.

Once a scanner identifies an open port, banner grabbing is used to gather additional information about the service or application running on that port.

Think of it as reading the sign or label on the door you just knocked on to understand what lies beyond.

Banner grabbing involves making a connection to the open port and capturing the banner or greeting message that the service sends when a connection is established.

This banner often contains valuable information such as the service name, version, and sometimes even details about the operating system running on the target system.

For example, when connecting to an FTP server, the banner may reveal that it's running vsftpd version 3.0.3 on a Linux system.

Why is banner grabbing important? Well, it provides attackers with insight into the specific software and versions running on a target system.

This information can be critical in identifying known vulnerabilities or weaknesses that can be exploited.

However, banner grabbing isn't solely the domain of attackers.

Ethical hackers and security professionals also use it to assess the security of their own systems.

By understanding what information can be obtained through banner grabbing, organizations can take proactive steps to secure their networked services.

Now, you might be wondering about the ethics of port scanning and banner grabbing.

Is it okay to probe other people's doors, even if they're left open?

The answer lies in the context and intent.

When conducted without authorization, port scanning and banner grabbing can be considered intrusive and potentially illegal.

Unauthorized scanning can disrupt services, violate privacy, and even lead to legal consequences.

However, when performed within the boundaries of ethical hacking, security assessments, or legitimate system administration, these techniques serve the vital purpose of identifying and addressing vulnerabilities before malicious actors can exploit them.

It's important to note that obtaining proper authorization and consent is paramount when conducting any form of network scanning or security assessment.

Responsible and ethical use of these techniques is essential to maintain trust and integrity within the cybersecurity community.

To recap, port scanning is like knocking on doors to identify open ports, while banner grabbing is akin to reading the labels on those doors to understand what's behind them.

Together, they form a powerful duo for assessing the security posture of networked systems.

When used responsibly and with proper authorization, these techniques play a crucial role in defending against cyber threats and safeguarding the digital world.

Let's embark on a journey into the world of network enumeration—a process that involves uncovering the services and users residing within a network.

Imagine a network as a vast city with numerous buildings, each containing rooms filled with people and various activities.

Network enumeration is like exploring this city, discovering what services are available and identifying who the inhabitants are.

Understanding the services and users in a network is crucial for various reasons, including security assessments, system administration, and troubleshooting.

When conducting network enumeration, one of the first steps is to discover the live hosts or devices on the network.

This process involves sending out probes or "pings" to IP addresses within a specified range to determine which hosts are reachable and responsive.

Live host discovery helps narrow down the scope of enumeration efforts, ensuring that you focus on active devices.

Once live hosts are identified, the next step is to enumerate the open ports on each device.

Ports act as entry points or doors to services and applications within a host.

By identifying open ports, you gain insight into which services are running and accessible on each device.

Port scanning techniques, such as the SYN scan or UDP scan, can be employed to determine the status of ports.

The results of port scanning reveal valuable information about the services offered by each host.

Imagine discovering a building with several doors, each leading to a different service—a web server, an email server, or a database server.

Port scanning helps you identify which doors are open and ready for interaction.

Banner grabbing, as we discussed earlier, plays a significant role in this process.

Once you identify an open port, you can attempt to connect to it and capture the banner or greeting message.

The banner often discloses information about the service, including its name, version, and sometimes even the operating system it's running on.

Banner grabbing is like reading the labels on the doors of the building to understand what lies behind each one.

Knowing the services running on each host is valuable, but network enumeration goes beyond that.

It's also crucial to enumerate the users and accounts within the network.

User enumeration involves identifying valid usernames, which can be used for various purposes, including unauthorized access attempts.

Common methods for user enumeration include using brute-force techniques, exploiting vulnerabilities, or leveraging misconfigurations.

Brute-force attacks involve systematically trying different usernames and passwords until a valid combination is found. Enumeration tools and scripts can automate this process, making it more efficient for attackers.

However, ethical hackers and security professionals also use brute-force techniques to identify weak passwords and bolster security.

Exploiting vulnerabilities or misconfigurations can also lead to user enumeration.

For example, a misconfigured web application may reveal user account information when manipulated in a specific way.

By identifying users within the network, security professionals can assess the strength of authentication mechanisms and recommend improvements.

Enumeration efforts can also reveal information about group memberships, permissions, and privileges associated with user accounts.

This knowledge is vital for understanding the network's access control structure and potential security risks.

For example, identifying a user with administrative privileges provides valuable insights into who has the authority to make critical changes within the network.

Enumeration can also uncover hidden or obscure services and accounts that may not be immediately apparent.

For instance, some devices or applications might run services on non-standard ports to evade detection.

Discovering these hidden services is essential for a comprehensive understanding of the network.

While network enumeration is a valuable process, it's essential to conduct it responsibly and within the bounds of ethical hacking and security assessments.

Unauthorized enumeration attempts can disrupt services, violate privacy, and even lead to legal consequences.

Obtaining proper authorization and consent is a fundamental principle when conducting any form of network enumeration.

Additionally, organizations should employ security measures to defend against enumeration attempts.

These measures include intrusion detection systems, firewalls, and network monitoring tools that can detect and alert administrators to suspicious activities.

Security policies should also be in place to govern the conduct of network enumeration and define acceptable and unacceptable practices.

In summary, network enumeration is a crucial aspect of understanding the services and users within a network.

It's akin to exploring a city, discovering the buildings, services, and inhabitants that make up the network landscape.

When conducted responsibly and ethically, network enumeration is a powerful tool for security assessments, system administration, and troubleshooting, helping organizations better protect their digital infrastructure.

Chapter 9: Vulnerability Assessment

Let's dive into the realm of cybersecurity once more and explore the crucial process of identifying and prioritizing vulnerabilities in digital systems and networks.

Imagine you're the captain of a ship, sailing through uncharted waters.

To navigate safely, you need to know where the treacherous rocks and hidden obstacles are.

In the world of cybersecurity, systems and networks are like ships, and vulnerabilities are the hidden dangers that threaten their security.

Identifying vulnerabilities is the first step in ensuring the safety of your digital journey.

Vulnerabilities can take various forms, including software bugs, misconfigurations, weak passwords, or flawed network design.

They are the weak points that attackers seek to exploit.

To identify vulnerabilities, cybersecurity professionals employ a variety of methods and tools.

One common approach is vulnerability scanning.

This involves using automated scanning tools to systematically examine systems and networks for known vulnerabilities.

Think of it as sending out scouts to search for hidden dangers beneath the surface.

These tools compare the configuration and software versions of systems against a database of known vulnerabilities.

If a match is found, it means there's a potential weakness that needs attention.

Another method for identifying vulnerabilities is manual testing or penetration testing.

In this approach, cybersecurity experts take on the role of ethical hackers, actively probing systems and networks for weaknesses.

They employ a combination of techniques, including network scanning, vulnerability scanning, and manual analysis, to uncover vulnerabilities that may not be detected by automated tools.

Imagine these experts as experienced explorers, carefully examining every nook and cranny for hidden dangers.

Furthermore, threat intelligence plays a crucial role in identifying vulnerabilities.

Cybersecurity professionals continuously monitor sources of information about emerging threats and vulnerabilities in the digital landscape.

These sources include security advisories, hacker forums, and research from security organizations.

By staying informed about the latest developments, organizations can proactively identify vulnerabilities that may be exploited by attackers.

Once vulnerabilities are identified, the next step is prioritization.

Imagine you've found a map with multiple danger zones marked, but you can't address all of them at once.

Prioritization helps you decide where to focus your efforts first.

Not all vulnerabilities are created equal; some pose a higher risk than others.

Prioritization is based on several factors, including the severity of the vulnerability, the potential impact on the organization, and the likelihood of exploitation.

A common framework for prioritizing vulnerabilities is the Common Vulnerability Scoring System (CVSS), which assigns a score to each vulnerability based on its characteristics.

The CVSS score takes into account factors such as the exploitability of the vulnerability, the impact on confidentiality, integrity, and availability, and whether there are known exploits in the wild.

Imagine these factors as different weights on a scale, helping you determine the overall risk posed by each vulnerability.

High-severity vulnerabilities with a high likelihood of exploitation and a significant impact on the organization are typically addressed first.

These are the equivalent of imminent dangers that need immediate attention.

Medium-severity vulnerabilities may be addressed next, followed by low-severity ones.

It's important to note that not all vulnerabilities need to be patched or mitigated immediately.

Some vulnerabilities may be less critical due to compensating controls, network segmentation, or other security measures in place.

Prioritization allows organizations to allocate resources effectively and address the most pressing security concerns first.

Once vulnerabilities are prioritized, the next step is remediation.

Remediation involves taking action to mitigate or eliminate the vulnerabilities identified.

This can include applying patches, reconfiguring systems, strengthening passwords, or implementing security measures to reduce the risk.

Imagine these actions as building barricades to protect against potential dangers.

Patch management is a critical aspect of vulnerability remediation.

Software vendors regularly release patches to address known vulnerabilities.

Organizations should have a robust patch management process in place to promptly apply patches to vulnerable systems.

Additionally, vulnerability remediation may involve changes to network configurations, access controls, or security policies.

These measures help fortify the digital defenses, reducing the risk of exploitation.

Furthermore, organizations should monitor and verify the effectiveness of their remediation efforts.

This involves testing systems to ensure that vulnerabilities have been successfully addressed and that no new issues have arisen as a result of remediation.

Monitoring is like keeping an eye on the horizon, ensuring that the ship remains on a safe course.

Regular vulnerability assessments, penetration testing, and continuous monitoring help organizations maintain a proactive stance against evolving threats.

In the ever-changing cybersecurity landscape, new vulnerabilities are discovered, and attackers continually adapt their tactics.

Therefore, the process of identifying, prioritizing, and remediating vulnerabilities should be ongoing and integrated into the organization's cybersecurity strategy.

In summary, identifying and prioritizing vulnerabilities is a vital aspect of cybersecurity.

It's like mapping out the hidden dangers in the digital landscape and deciding where to fortify your defenses first.

By following a systematic approach and staying vigilant, organizations can strengthen their security posture and navigate the digital seas with confidence.

Let's delve into the intriguing world of penetration testing— a crucial practice in cybersecurity that goes beyond identifying vulnerabilities to actively validate their existence and assess the resilience of a system or network against real-world attacks.

Imagine you're an architect designing a fortress, and you want to ensure its defenses are impregnable.

To do so, you don't just rely on blueprints and theoretical knowledge; you conduct practical tests to ensure that your design can withstand actual threats.

Similarly, in the realm of cybersecurity, penetration testing serves as the practical test that validates the security measures in place.

Penetration testing, often referred to as pen testing or ethical hacking, is the process of simulating real-world cyberattacks to evaluate the security of a system, network, or application.

It's like stress-testing a bridge to make sure it won't collapse under heavy loads.

The goal is to identify vulnerabilities and weaknesses that malicious actors could exploit, understand the potential impact of these vulnerabilities, and validate the effectiveness of security controls.

Penetration testers, also known as ethical hackers, conduct these tests with the explicit permission of the organization to ensure that the assessments are conducted legally and responsibly.

Think of them as friendly invaders, probing the digital fortifications to help strengthen them.

The first step in penetration testing is defining the scope of the test.

This includes identifying the target systems, networks, or applications that will be assessed, as well as the specific goals and objectives of the test.

Imagine this as mapping out the boundaries of the digital battlefield to ensure that the testing is focused and controlled.

Once the scope is defined, the penetration tester begins the reconnaissance phase.

During this phase, they gather information about the target, such as IP addresses, domain names, and potential vulnerabilities.

This information is essential for planning the attack, just as a military strategist would gather intelligence about an enemy's positions and weaknesses before launching an assault.

The reconnaissance phase can involve passive information gathering, such as collecting publicly available data, or active techniques, such as network scanning and enumeration.

Imagine it as spies collecting critical data to plan their mission.

With reconnaissance complete, the penetration tester moves on to the actual exploitation phase.

This is where they attempt to exploit the identified vulnerabilities to gain unauthorized access, escalate privileges, or perform other malicious actions that an attacker might attempt.

It's like trying to breach the fortress walls by finding weak points in the defenses.

Common techniques used during this phase include password cracking, exploiting software vulnerabilities, and leveraging misconfigurations.

The goal is not just to prove that vulnerabilities exist but to demonstrate the potential impact of a successful attack.

For example, gaining access to sensitive data or taking control of a critical system.

It's the equivalent of showing that the fortress can be breached and the enemy can take control if the defenses are not strong enough.

Throughout the exploitation phase, the penetration tester meticulously documents their actions and findings.

This documentation is essential for the organization to understand how the attack was carried out, what vulnerabilities were exploited, and what data or systems were compromised.

Imagine it as creating a detailed report of the battle, including tactics, vulnerabilities, and outcomes.

Once the exploitation phase is complete, the penetration tester moves on to post-exploitation activities.

This involves maintaining access to the compromised systems, pivoting to other systems within the network, and further exploring the extent of the potential damage.

It's like infiltrating deeper into the enemy's territory once you've breached their defenses.

The post-exploitation phase helps the organization understand the full scope of the potential impact and assess the resilience of their security controls.

Throughout the entire penetration testing process, ethical hackers follow a strict code of ethics.

They ensure that they don't cause harm, disrupt business operations, or steal sensitive information.

Their goal is to identify and validate vulnerabilities, not to compromise the integrity or confidentiality of the organization's data.

Once the testing is complete, the penetration tester delivers a comprehensive report to the organization.

This report includes detailed findings, the techniques and tools used, the impact of successful attacks, and recommendations for remediation.

Imagine it as a battle report delivered to the fortress owner, outlining the vulnerabilities that were exposed and how to reinforce the defenses.

The organization can then use the findings to prioritize and address the identified vulnerabilities.

This might involve patching software, reconfiguring systems, strengthening access controls, or improving security awareness and training.

The ultimate goal is to fortify the digital defenses and reduce the risk of real-world attacks.

In summary, penetration testing is a vital practice in cybersecurity, akin to stress-testing digital fortifications to ensure they can withstand real-world threats.

Ethical hackers play a critical role in this process, simulating attacks to identify and validate vulnerabilities while adhering to a strict code of ethics.

The insights gained from penetration testing empower organizations to bolster their security measures, ultimately ensuring that their digital fortresses remain impregnable in the face of potential adversaries.

Chapter 10: Ethical Considerations in Information Gathering

Let's explore the intricate and crucial topic of legal and ethical frameworks within the realm of ethical hacking, where navigating the complex web of laws and moral principles is essential for ensuring the responsible and legitimate practice of cybersecurity.

Imagine you're an ethical hacker, armed with the knowledge and skills to uncover vulnerabilities and protect digital assets.

Just like a vigilant guardian, your mission is to defend against cyber threats while adhering to a set of rules and principles that govern your actions.

At the heart of ethical hacking lies the need to strike a delicate balance between probing for security weaknesses and respecting the rights and privacy of individuals and organizations.

To embark on this journey, you need to be well-versed in the legal and ethical frameworks that define the boundaries of your practice.

Legal frameworks serve as the guiding laws and regulations that dictate what is permissible and what is prohibited in the world of ethical hacking.

These laws can vary significantly from one jurisdiction to another, making it essential for ethical hackers to understand and comply with the specific regulations in their region.

Imagine these legal frameworks as the rules of engagement that ensure ethical hacking is conducted within the bounds of the law.

One of the fundamental legal principles in ethical hacking is obtaining proper authorization.

Before conducting any security assessment or penetration testing, ethical hackers must seek explicit permission from the owner or administrator of the system or network being tested.

This authorization, often in the form of a written agreement or contract, outlines the scope, objectives, and constraints of the testing.

Imagine it as a formal invitation to explore and assess the security of a digital asset.

Without proper authorization, ethical hacking activities can cross into the realm of illegal hacking, potentially resulting in criminal charges, civil lawsuits, or other legal consequences.

Another critical aspect of legal frameworks is the distinction between ethical hacking and malicious hacking.

Ethical hackers engage in cybersecurity practices with the intent of improving security, identifying vulnerabilities, and protecting digital assets.

Malicious hackers, on the other hand, exploit vulnerabilities for personal gain, causing harm or financial losses.

It's important to understand that even with good intentions, ethical hackers must tread carefully within the legal boundaries to avoid being mistaken for malicious actors.

Imagine it as the difference between a vigilant security guard and an intruder in the eyes of the law.

Data protection and privacy laws are also central to ethical hacking.

These laws govern the handling of sensitive information and personal data, ensuring that it is collected, stored, and processed responsibly and securely.

Ethical hackers must be well-versed in these laws, especially when conducting assessments that involve the handling of potentially sensitive data.

Imagine it as respecting the privacy of individuals and their personal information, just as you would want your own data to be protected.

Now, let's shift our focus to the ethical frameworks that guide ethical hacking practices.

Ethical frameworks are a set of moral principles and guidelines that dictate the right and wrong conduct in the field of cybersecurity.

They serve as the compass that helps ethical hackers navigate the ethical dilemmas and challenges they may encounter.

One of the foundational ethical principles in ethical hacking is integrity.

Ethical hackers must maintain honesty and transparency in their actions, providing accurate and unbiased assessments of vulnerabilities and risks.

Imagine it as a commitment to truthfulness and trustworthiness in the pursuit of cybersecurity.

Professionalism is another critical ethical principle.

Ethical hackers should conduct themselves in a professional manner, respecting the confidentiality of their findings and adhering to a strict code of conduct.

Imagine it as upholding a high standard of conduct and competence in every aspect of your work.

Respect for individuals' privacy and rights is paramount.

Ethical hackers must ensure that their assessments do not infringe on the privacy and rights of individuals or organizations.

Imagine it as treating others' digital properties and information with the same respect you would expect for your own.

Transparency and accountability are key ethical principles in ethical hacking.

Ethical hackers should be transparent about their methods, findings, and limitations, and they should be accountable for their actions and decisions.

Imagine it as being open and answerable for the choices you make in the pursuit of ethical hacking.

Now, imagine you're faced with an ethical dilemma during a penetration test.

You discover a critical vulnerability that, if exploited, could result in significant damage to the organization.

However, you also uncover evidence of potentially illegal activities within the organization.

Here's where the ethical frameworks come into play.

Ethical hackers must balance their responsibility to disclose and mitigate the vulnerability with their duty to respect the law and confidentiality.

In such situations, it's essential to consult with legal and ethical experts and consider the potential consequences of your actions.

Imagine it as weighing the ethical principles and making a well-informed decision that aligns with both the law and your moral values.

In summary, legal and ethical frameworks are the guiding lights that ensure the responsible and legitimate practice of ethical hacking.

They provide the rules of engagement and the moral compass that ethical hackers rely on to navigate the complex landscape of cybersecurity.

By adhering to these frameworks, ethical hackers can protect digital assets, uncover vulnerabilities, and uphold the highest standards of integrity and professionalism in their noble quest to defend against cyber threats.

Let's delve into the essential practice of responsible disclosure—a vital process that allows ethical hackers and security researchers to report vulnerabilities they discover to the affected organizations in a manner that promotes cybersecurity without causing harm.

Imagine you stumble upon a hidden passage in a fortress's wall, a vulnerability that could potentially be exploited by malicious intruders.

You have a moral duty to report this discovery to the fortress's owner, ensuring that the vulnerability is addressed promptly.

In the world of cybersecurity, responsible disclosure follows a similar principle.

It's the ethical and responsible way to handle vulnerabilities and security issues when they are found.

Responsible disclosure begins with the discovery of a vulnerability or security issue by an ethical hacker, security researcher, or concerned individual.

This discovery could be the result of proactive security assessments, such as penetration testing or vulnerability scanning, or it may arise incidentally during routine use of a system or application.

Imagine it as finding a hidden trapdoor that could lead to unauthorized access.

Once a vulnerability is discovered, the first step is to verify its existence and assess its severity.

Ethical hackers and security researchers rigorously test and validate the vulnerability to ensure it's not a false positive.

This verification process involves attempting to exploit the vulnerability to understand its impact fully.

Imagine it as testing the hidden trapdoor to confirm that it indeed leads to a sensitive area.

With a confirmed vulnerability in hand, the ethical hacker or researcher's next responsibility is to notify the organization or vendor that is affected.

This notification is typically done through a secure and confidential communication channel.

Imagine it as delivering a discreet message to the fortress owner, informing them of the hidden passage.

One crucial aspect of responsible disclosure is providing clear and detailed information about the vulnerability.

This includes a comprehensive description of the issue, the potential impact it could have, and steps to reproduce the vulnerability.

Imagine it as giving the fortress owner precise instructions on how to locate and secure the hidden passage.

Moreover, responsible disclosure often includes a timeline for the organization to address the vulnerability.

This timeline should be reasonable, allowing the organization sufficient time to develop and implement a fix while minimizing the risk of exploitation.

Imagine it as giving the fortress owner a deadline to seal the hidden passage before disclosing it to the public.

During this period, the ethical hacker or researcher may work collaboratively with the organization's security team to provide additional information, guidance, and assistance in mitigating the vulnerability.

Imagine it as sharing expertise on fortification techniques to help secure the hidden passage.

Now, let's address the concept of coordinated disclosure.

Coordinated disclosure is a collaborative approach that involves multiple parties, including the organization, the ethical hacker or researcher, and sometimes even cybersecurity experts and government agencies.

Imagine it as inviting skilled locksmiths to assess the hidden passage and provide recommendations for reinforcement.

The goal of coordinated disclosure is to ensure that vulnerabilities are addressed efficiently and responsibly.

It allows organizations to benefit from the expertise of ethical hackers and researchers while minimizing the risk of potential exploitation.

Imagine it as involving a team of experts to secure the hidden passage comprehensively.

However, not all organizations respond promptly or adequately to vulnerability reports.

In some cases, ethical hackers and researchers encounter resistance, indifference, or a lack of action from the organization.

When this happens, the responsible disclosure process may escalate to public disclosure, a step taken when the organization fails to address the vulnerability within a reasonable timeframe.

Public disclosure involves sharing information about the vulnerability with the broader cybersecurity community and the public.

Imagine it as publishing the location of the hidden passage for all to see.

Public disclosure can exert pressure on the organization to take the issue seriously and prompt them to address the vulnerability promptly.

However, it's a step that should be taken with caution and as a last resort.

The goal of responsible disclosure is not to harm the organization but to protect digital assets and enhance cybersecurity.

Imagine it as a responsible guardian of the fortress who resorts to publicly disclosing the hidden passage only when all other attempts to secure it have failed.

Responsible disclosure is a practice rooted in ethics and integrity.

It upholds the principles of transparency, collaboration, and the greater good of cybersecurity.

Imagine it as a commitment to safeguarding the digital realm by responsibly sharing knowledge about vulnerabilities.

In summary, responsible disclosure is the ethical and responsible way to handle vulnerabilities in the cybersecurity landscape.

It's akin to discovering a hidden passage in a fortress and ensuring that the fortress owner is informed and given an opportunity to secure it.

By following the principles of responsible disclosure, ethical hackers and security researchers contribute to a safer digital world, where vulnerabilities are addressed, and cyber threats are mitigated responsibly and without harm.

BOOK 2
MASTERING FOOTPRINTING
ADVANCED INFORMATION GATHERING STRATEGIES FOR
ETHICAL HACKERS

ROB BOTWRIGHT

Chapter 1: Advanced Footprinting Techniques

Let's explore the fascinating world of Passive DNS Enumeration and Analysis, a powerful technique in the realm of cybersecurity that provides valuable insights into the historical and current domain name system (DNS) activity without directly querying DNS servers.

Imagine you're a detective investigating a complex case, and you need to uncover the history of a suspect's movements and activities without alerting them.

This is somewhat analogous to the concept of Passive DNS Enumeration and Analysis, where you gather critical information about domains and their associations without actively querying DNS servers.

The Domain Name System (DNS) serves as the internet's phone book, translating human-friendly domain names into IP addresses that computers can understand.

It's the backbone of internet communication, allowing us to access websites, send emails, and perform countless online activities.

Passive DNS Enumeration and Analysis, also known as Passive DNS, is a technique that leverages DNS data collected from various sources to build a historical record of DNS resolutions and mappings.

Imagine it as a detailed timeline of internet domain activity, showing when and where each domain pointed to over time.

Now, let's dive into the process of Passive DNS Enumeration and Analysis.

It begins with the collection of DNS data from a variety of sources, including DNS resolvers, DNS traffic captures, and DNS query logs.

This data can come from various locations on the internet, such as ISPs, organizations, and researchers who collect and store DNS information.

Imagine these sources as data collectors scattered across the digital landscape, silently recording DNS activity.

The collected DNS data is then processed and analyzed to extract valuable information.

One of the primary pieces of information gathered through Passive DNS is the historical resolution data for domain names.

This data shows the different IP addresses that a domain has pointed to over time, revealing changes in hosting or infrastructure.

Imagine it as tracking the different addresses where a suspect has lived or visited over the years.

Another essential aspect of Passive DNS Analysis is the identification of subdomains associated with a domain.

This information can be useful for understanding the structure of a website or identifying potentially malicious subdomains.

Imagine it as discovering hidden rooms or compartments within a suspect's residence.

Passive DNS also provides insights into the timeframes during which DNS records were observed.

This temporal information can be critical for understanding the evolution of a domain's activity, including when it was first registered, when it became active, and when it may have changed ownership.

Imagine it as a timeline of events in the life of a domain, like entries in a suspect's diary.

The Passive DNS process helps cybersecurity professionals, incident responders, and researchers uncover valuable information about domains and their associations.

For example, it can be used to investigate malicious domains used in cyberattacks.

Imagine it as following the breadcrumbs left by a criminal, piecing together their activities and connections.

Passive DNS can also assist in identifying potentially compromised systems or tracking the movement of malicious infrastructure.

Imagine it as tracing the path of a cybercriminal on a digital map.

Moreover, Passive DNS Enumeration and Analysis play a vital role in threat intelligence and threat hunting.

By examining DNS data, organizations and security experts can proactively identify and respond to emerging threats.

Imagine it as having a proactive strategy to prevent crimes before they occur.

To further illustrate the value of Passive DNS, let's consider an example.

Suppose a cybersecurity analyst is investigating a suspected phishing campaign targeting a particular organization.

They have identified a phishing domain used in the campaign but want to gather more information about its infrastructure and other associated domains.

By leveraging Passive DNS Enumeration and Analysis, the analyst can retrieve historical DNS resolution data for the suspicious domain.

They discover that the domain was recently registered and has pointed to multiple IP addresses in a short period, suggesting potentially malicious activity.

Furthermore, the analyst identifies several subdomains associated with the phishing domain, some of which appear to mimic legitimate services of the targeted organization.

With this information, the analyst can take appropriate actions, such as blocking access to the phishing domain and notifying the organization's incident response team.

Imagine it as the detective unraveling a complex web of clues to solve a case and protect potential victims.

In summary, Passive DNS Enumeration and Analysis is a valuable tool in the cybersecurity arsenal.

It allows for the gathering of historical and current DNS data without directly querying DNS servers, providing insights into domain activity and associations.

Just like a detective piecing together a puzzle, cybersecurity professionals use Passive DNS to uncover valuable information about domains, track malicious infrastructure, and proactively defend against cyber threats.

Let's embark on a journey into the fascinating world of geolocation and IP tracking methods, where technology enables us to pinpoint the physical location of devices connected to the internet, offering valuable insights for various applications.

Imagine you're equipped with a digital map, and you have the ability to identify the precise location of any device connected to the internet, much like finding a hidden treasure with a virtual treasure map.

Geolocation and IP tracking make this concept a reality, providing a range of tools and techniques to determine the geographical coordinates of devices, such as computers, smartphones, and IoT devices, based on their IP addresses.

At its core, geolocation relies on the global infrastructure of the internet, which routes data packets between devices using a system of IP addresses.

Every device connected to the internet is assigned a unique IP address, serving as its digital identifier.

Imagine it as an address for each device in the vast neighborhood of the internet.

Now, let's explore the methods and technologies used for geolocation and IP tracking.

One common approach is known as IP address geolocation, which relies on databases containing information about the geographical locations associated with specific IP address ranges.

Imagine it as a massive address book mapping IP addresses to physical locations.

These databases are continually updated and refined, allowing for increasingly accurate geolocation results.

Another method involves using GPS data from devices with built-in GPS receivers, such as smartphones and some laptops.

This data can be used to determine the device's location with high precision.

Imagine it as tracing a device's exact position on Earth using satellites.

Additionally, Wi-Fi geolocation utilizes information from nearby Wi-Fi access points to triangulate a device's position.

When a device scans for available Wi-Fi networks, it can detect the names (SSIDs) and signal strengths of nearby access points.

By comparing this information with a database of known Wi-Fi access points and their locations, the device can estimate its own position.

Imagine it as a device identifying landmarks by the strength of nearby radio signals.

Cellular tower triangulation is another method, commonly used by mobile network providers to determine the approximate location of a mobile device.

When a device connects to a cellular network, it communicates with nearby cell towers.

By analyzing the signal strength and timing of these communications, the network can estimate the device's location.

Imagine it as a device pinpointing its position based on its conversations with nearby cellular towers.

IP tracking also involves using web-based services and tools that collect information about a device's IP address when it interacts with websites or online services.

Imagine it as a device revealing its location when it visits a digital store or café on the internet.

Moreover, browser-based geolocation leverages HTML5's Geolocation API, which allows websites to request the device's location with the user's consent.

This method uses a combination of GPS data, Wi-Fi information, and IP address data to provide a highly accurate location.

Imagine it as a website politely asking for directions, and the device willingly shares its coordinates.

While geolocation and IP tracking have numerous practical applications, such as helping users find nearby restaurants or assisting emergency services in locating callers, they also raise important privacy considerations.

Imagine it as a balance between convenience and safeguarding personal information.

Privacy-conscious individuals may be concerned about the potential misuse of their location data.

To address these concerns, various safeguards and regulations are in place.

For example, many websites and apps require user consent before accessing location information.

Imagine it as asking for permission before using someone's map to find a treasure.

Furthermore, there are legal frameworks, such as the General Data Protection Regulation (GDPR) in Europe, that impose strict rules on how organizations collect, store, and use location data.

Imagine it as establishing rules and guidelines to protect the treasure map and its owner.

As we navigate the world of geolocation and IP tracking, it's important to recognize that these technologies have transformed how we interact with digital services and the physical world.

They enable innovative applications like ride-sharing services, location-based advertising, and asset tracking.

Imagine it as a digital compass guiding us through a modern treasure hunt.

In the realm of cybersecurity, geolocation and IP tracking can also play a vital role.

Security professionals may use these techniques to investigate and respond to cyber threats.

Imagine it as tracing the path of a digital intruder back to their origin.

For instance, if a security system detects unusual activity from a specific IP address, geolocation can help determine the physical location of the potentially compromised device.

Imagine it as identifying the location of a suspect in a digital investigation.

In summary, geolocation and IP tracking methods have become integral to our connected world, offering valuable insights and convenience while also raising privacy and security considerations.

They empower us to find the hidden treasures of digital services and navigate the landscape of cyberspace with precision.

By understanding these technologies and their implications, we can strike a balance between harnessing their benefits and safeguarding our privacy and security in the digital age.

Chapter 2: Expanding OSINT Capabilities

Let's dive into the captivating realm of Advanced Open Source Intelligence (OSINT) tools and resources, where we explore a treasure trove of digital tools and techniques that empower researchers, investigators, and cybersecurity professionals to uncover hidden information and insights from publicly available sources.

Imagine embarking on a digital quest, armed with a set of advanced tools that act as a digital magnifying glass, revealing hidden details and connections within the vast landscape of online information.

These advanced OSINT tools and resources serve as indispensable companions on this journey, enhancing our ability to gather, analyze, and interpret data from the open web.

Open Source Intelligence (OSINT) is the practice of collecting and analyzing information from publicly accessible sources, such as websites, social media platforms, public records, and more.

It's akin to being an investigator who combs through public archives, newspapers, and interviews to piece together a puzzle.

In the digital age, OSINT has evolved, and advanced tools have emerged to aid in the discovery and extraction of valuable intelligence.

Let's start by delving into some of the advanced OSINT tools available today.

One prominent category of tools is web scraping and data extraction tools.

Imagine these tools as digital hands that can sift through web pages, extracting specific information, such as email addresses, phone numbers, or financial data.

They automate the process of data collection from websites, making it more efficient and comprehensive.

Another essential category is social media analysis tools.

These tools provide the capability to monitor and analyze social media platforms, where a wealth of information is shared by individuals and organizations.

Imagine them as lenses that allow you to focus on specific keywords, hashtags, or users to gather insights and detect trends.

Furthermore, there are OSINT tools designed for domain and IP investigation.

These tools enable users to uncover information about websites, domain ownership, and IP addresses.

Imagine them as digital detectives that unveil the hidden details of internet infrastructure.

Additionally, data enrichment tools play a vital role in OSINT.

They help enhance existing data by adding context and additional information.

Imagine them as puzzle pieces that complete the picture, making it more informative and actionable.

Geospatial intelligence tools are another valuable resource.

These tools allow users to analyze and visualize location-based data, such as maps, satellite imagery, and geographic information systems (GIS).

Imagine them as maps that help you navigate the terrain of geospatial information.

Moreover, there are tools specialized in monitoring and analyzing online forums and communities.

These tools are essential for tracking discussions, trends, and sentiments within specific online groups.

Imagine them as listening posts that tune in to digital conversations.

Furthermore, image and video analysis tools have become increasingly sophisticated.

They can analyze images and videos to extract valuable metadata, identify objects or faces, and even detect deepfake content.

Imagine them as digital eyes that scrutinize multimedia for hidden clues.

Now, let's explore some of the notable resources that complement these advanced OSINT tools.

First and foremost, open data repositories are invaluable.

Many governments and organizations provide access to vast datasets, ranging from demographic information to economic indicators.

Imagine them as treasure troves of structured data waiting to be explored.

Public records and archives are essential resources in OSINT.

These include documents like court records, business registrations, property records, and historical archives.

Imagine them as digital libraries filled with historical and factual records.

Academic and research databases offer a wealth of scholarly articles, papers, and publications.

Imagine them as libraries of knowledge, where you can find in-depth information on various subjects.

News aggregators and media outlets provide access to current events and news articles.

They are valuable for staying informed and tracking developments in real-time.

Imagine them as digital newspapers that deliver the latest headlines.

Online communities and forums can be rich sources of information and insights.

Engaging with these communities allows OSINT practitioners to tap into collective knowledge and expertise.

Imagine them as virtual gatherings of experts and enthusiasts.

Now, let's illustrate the practical use of advanced OSINT tools and resources with an example.

Imagine you are a cybersecurity analyst investigating a cyberattack on your organization.

You suspect that the attacker is using a specific malware variant.

To gather intelligence, you employ advanced OSINT tools to search for indicators of compromise (IOCs) associated with the malware.

Web scraping tools help you extract IOCs from security blogs, forums, and open-source reports.

Social media analysis tools allow you to monitor discussions related to the malware on Twitter and other platforms.

Domain and IP investigation tools help you uncover the infrastructure used by the attacker, while data enrichment tools provide additional context.

You also turn to geospatial intelligence tools to map out the geographic distribution of the attack.

Additionally, image and video analysis tools help you examine screenshots of the malware and analyze any multimedia elements associated with it.

Through these advanced OSINT tools and resources, you assemble a comprehensive picture of the cyberattack, its origins, and potential threat actors.

You can then take appropriate action to mitigate the attack and strengthen your organization's cybersecurity defenses.

In summary, advanced OSINT tools and resources empower individuals and organizations to extract valuable intelligence from publicly available sources in the digital age.

They serve as digital assistants in the quest for information, helping researchers, investigators, and cybersecurity professionals uncover hidden details and connections within the vast landscape of online data.

By harnessing the capabilities of these tools and resources, we can navigate the digital realm more effectively and make informed decisions based on actionable intelligence.

Let's embark on an exciting exploration of Geospatial Intelligence (GEOINT) within the realm of Open Source Intelligence (OSINT), a captivating intersection where location-based data and open-source information converge to provide valuable insights into the physical world around us.

Imagine you have a pair of magical glasses that allow you to see beyond what meets the eye, revealing hidden patterns, connections, and geographical details in the world's data.

This is akin to the power of GEOINT in OSINT, where technology transforms ordinary information into a powerful tool for understanding the spatial dimensions of our environment.

To begin, let's unravel the essence of GEOINT within OSINT.

Geospatial Intelligence (GEOINT) is the discipline of gathering, analyzing, and interpreting data related to the physical location and characteristics of objects, features, and events on Earth.

Imagine it as a multidimensional map, where every data point is not just a dot but a rich source of information about its geographical context.

In the context of OSINT, GEOINT involves harnessing publicly available geospatial data from sources like satellite imagery, aerial photographs, geographic information systems (GIS), maps, and location-based information.

These sources act as the building blocks of GEOINT, providing a foundation for understanding the world through a geographical lens.

Imagine it as assembling a digital jigsaw puzzle, where each piece represents a fragment of our physical reality.

Now, let's delve into the practical applications and tools that make GEOINT an indispensable component of OSINT.

One of the primary applications of GEOINT in OSINT is geolocation.

This involves determining the precise geographic location of a particular object, event, or even a person.

Imagine it as a digital GPS system that can pinpoint the exact coordinates of a hidden treasure or a missing person based on available data.

Satellite imagery plays a pivotal role in GEOINT.

Satellites orbiting the Earth capture high-resolution images of the planet's surface, which are accessible through open-source platforms like Google Earth and Sentinel Hub.

Imagine it as having access to a telescope that can peer down at any location on Earth, offering a bird's-eye view of landscapes, cities, and even remote areas.

Aerial photography complements satellite imagery.

It involves capturing images from aircraft flying at lower altitudes, providing detailed views of specific regions or objects.

Imagine it as using a drone to take photographs of a hidden archaeological site or a natural disaster's aftermath.

Geographic Information Systems (GIS) are fundamental to GEOINT.

These software systems allow users to collect, manage, analyze, and visualize geographical data.

Imagine it as a digital map-making toolkit that can layer information about land use, demographics, and environmental factors.

Maps, both traditional and digital, are essential tools in GEOINT.

They serve as visual representations of geographical data, making complex information more accessible and understandable.

Imagine it as having a roadmap to navigate through intricate terrains of data.

Location-based information from social media platforms is a treasure trove for GEOINT practitioners.

People often share their locations, activities, and experiences on platforms like Twitter, Instagram, and Foursquare.

Imagine it as listening to people's travel diaries, where they voluntarily provide insights about their whereabouts.

Crowdsourced mapping projects, such as OpenStreetMap, allow volunteers to contribute geographic data.

These community-driven efforts create detailed and up-to-date maps of various locations worldwide.

Imagine it as a collaborative painting where everyone adds strokes to create a collective masterpiece.

Furthermore, advanced analytics and machine learning algorithms have revolutionized GEOINT in OSINT.

They can process vast amounts of geospatial data, identify patterns, detect anomalies, and make predictions based on historical information.

Imagine it as having a team of digital analysts who can sift through mountains of data and provide meaningful insights.

Now, let's explore practical scenarios where GEOINT in OSINT shines.

Imagine you're an environmental researcher investigating deforestation in a remote rainforest.

You can use satellite imagery and GIS tools to monitor changes in forest cover, detect illegal logging activities, and assess the impact on biodiversity.

Imagine you're a humanitarian aid worker responding to a natural disaster.

Aerial imagery and GIS mapping help you identify areas of greatest need, plan evacuation routes, and coordinate relief efforts efficiently.

Imagine you're a journalist reporting on a conflict zone.

You can use geolocation and social media data to verify the authenticity of photos and videos, corroborate eyewitness accounts, and piece together the timeline of events.

Imagine you're a business owner looking to expand your market.

Location-based information can help you analyze customer demographics, assess the suitability of potential store locations, and optimize delivery routes.

Imagine you're a security analyst tracking the movements of a potential threat.

GEOINT allows you to monitor the movement patterns of individuals or groups, identify potential hotspots, and assess security risks.

Imagine you're an archaeologist exploring ancient civilizations.

Satellite imagery, aerial photography, and GIS mapping help you discover hidden archaeological sites, plan excavations, and reconstruct historical landscapes.

In summary, Geospatial Intelligence (GEOINT) within Open Source Intelligence (OSINT) is a potent tool that transforms ordinary data into a geographical treasure map.

It enables us to uncover hidden patterns, detect changes in the physical world, and make informed decisions about our environment.

By harnessing GEOINT in OSINT, we gain a deeper understanding of our world's spatial dimensions and unlock new insights for a wide range of applications, from environmental conservation to disaster response, journalism to business, security to archaeology.

Chapter 3: Web Application Reconnaissance

Let's embark on a fascinating journey into the world of crawling and mapping web applications, where we explore the intricate process of navigating the vast digital landscape of websites and online services, much like an intrepid explorer charting uncharted territory in the digital realm.

Imagine you're equipped with a sophisticated digital compass and a detailed map of the internet, ready to navigate the complex terrain of web applications, each one a unique ecosystem of interconnected pages and functionalities.

This is the essence of crawling and mapping web applications, a critical aspect of cybersecurity, website optimization, and data analysis.

To begin, let's unravel the concept of web crawling and its significance.

Web crawling is the process of systematically traversing the web, visiting web pages, and collecting data from them.

Imagine it as sending out a fleet of digital scouts to explore the vast landscape of the internet, meticulously cataloging the information they encounter along the way.

Crawling is typically performed by automated software programs called web crawlers or spiders.

These digital explorers follow hyperlinks from one web page to another, indexing content, and collecting data such as text, images, metadata, and more.

Imagine it as a team of digital archaeologists excavating information buried within the web's intricate layers.

Now, let's delve into the practical aspects of web crawling and its significance in various domains.

Web crawlers are employed by search engines like Google, Bing, and Yahoo to index web pages, making them searchable.

Imagine it as the indexing system of a vast library, ensuring that every book (web page) is categorized and accessible to those seeking information.

In the realm of website optimization, web crawlers help website owners and administrators identify issues, such as broken links, missing pages, or duplicate content.

Imagine them as digital inspectors, scanning a website's structure to ensure it's well-maintained and user-friendly.

Moreover, web crawlers play a vital role in data mining and data extraction.

They can be used to collect valuable information from websites, ranging from product prices and reviews to news articles and social media posts.

Imagine them as digital miners extracting precious nuggets of data from the web's information-rich deposits.

In cybersecurity, web application scanning and vulnerability assessment rely on web crawling techniques.

Security professionals use web crawlers to identify potential security flaws or vulnerabilities in web applications, helping organizations safeguard their digital assets.

Imagine them as digital sentinels patrolling the virtual walls, searching for weak points that hackers might exploit.

Now, let's shift our focus to the mapping aspect of web applications.

Mapping web applications involves creating a visual representation of a website's structure, including its pages, navigation paths, and interactions.

Imagine it as crafting a detailed blueprint of a complex building, showing every room, corridor, and connection.

One common way to map web applications is through the use of sitemaps.

A sitemap is a hierarchical list or diagram that outlines the structure of a website, including its main pages, subpages, and their relationships.

Imagine it as a digital floor plan that helps users and search engines navigate a website efficiently.

Web application mapping tools and software can automatically generate sitemaps, making the process more efficient for website owners and administrators.

Imagine them as digital architects who can quickly design and update the blueprints of a website.

Furthermore, interactive mapping tools allow users to visualize the user interface (UI) and user experience (UX) of a web application.

These tools help designers and developers understand how users will interact with the application, leading to more user-friendly designs.

Imagine them as virtual tour guides, showcasing the flow and functionality of a website.

In cybersecurity, mapping web applications is crucial for identifying potential attack surfaces and vulnerabilities.

By comprehensively understanding the structure and functionality of a web application, security professionals can assess its security posture and develop strategies to protect it.

Imagine it as mapping the layout of a fortress to identify potential weaknesses in its defenses.

To illustrate the practicality of crawling and mapping web applications, let's consider an example.

Imagine you are a cybersecurity analyst tasked with assessing the security of an e-commerce website.

Your goal is to identify potential vulnerabilities that could be exploited by malicious actors.

You start by using a web crawler to systematically explore the website's pages and functionalities.

The crawler follows links, collects data on input fields, and analyzes the behavior of forms and buttons.

As it traverses the website, it logs its findings, such as potential entry points for SQL injection or cross-site scripting (XSS) attacks.

Next, you use a web application mapping tool to create a visual map of the website's structure.

The map highlights the interconnectedness of pages, user flows, and data interactions.

You identify areas of the application where sensitive user data is processed and stored, making them potential targets for attackers.

By combining the insights from crawling and mapping, you develop a comprehensive security assessment report.

This report includes recommendations for mitigating vulnerabilities, securing data inputs, and enhancing overall web application security.

In summary, crawling and mapping web applications are essential processes in the digital landscape, serving diverse purposes from information retrieval to security assessment.

They enable us to navigate the complex terrain of the internet, extract valuable data, optimize websites, and enhance cybersecurity measures.

Much like digital cartographers and explorers, we rely on these techniques to chart our course and uncover hidden treasures in the vast realm of web applications.

Let's delve into the intriguing world of fingerprinting server-side technologies, a fascinating journey where we uncover the digital signatures left behind by web servers and the software powering them, much like a detective examining clues at a crime scene.

Imagine you are a cyber sleuth armed with the tools to unveil the hidden identity of web servers, discerning the software, versions, and configurations that define their digital personalities.

This is the essence of server-side technology fingerprinting, a crucial aspect of cybersecurity, web development, and digital forensics.

To start, let's demystify the concept of server-side technology fingerprinting and why it matters.

Server-side technology fingerprinting, also known as server fingerprinting or banner grabbing, is the process of identifying the software and specific versions running on a web server by analyzing the responses it provides when queried.

Think of it as an investigator examining a suspect's attire, mannerisms, and speech to determine their identity; in the digital realm, we analyze the responses of web servers to uncover their underlying technologies.

This process involves sending specific requests to web servers and closely inspecting the responses they return.

Now, let's explore the significance and applications of server-side technology fingerprinting in various domains.

In cybersecurity, server-side technology fingerprinting is a vital reconnaissance technique.

Security professionals use it to gather intelligence about the software stack used by a web server, which can help identify potential vulnerabilities and security weaknesses.

Imagine it as scanning an enemy's armor to find weak points before engaging in battle.

Web developers and administrators employ server-side technology fingerprinting to assess and manage their server infrastructure.

By knowing the software and versions in use, they can apply patches, updates, and configuration changes to maintain a secure and efficient web environment.

Think of it as a mechanic identifying the make and model of a car to perform maintenance tasks effectively.

Digital forensics experts use server-side technology fingerprinting to investigate cyber incidents.

When analyzing network traffic or compromised servers, they can determine the technologies involved, aiding in the attribution of cyberattacks and the reconstruction of digital crime scenes.

Imagine it as piecing together evidence from a crime scene to solve a mystery.

Now, let's delve into the practical aspects of server-side technology fingerprinting.

One common technique is examining the HTTP response headers sent by web servers.

These headers contain valuable information about the server, such as the server software, version, and even the operating system.

Imagine it as reading the identification badge of a person to learn their name and occupation.

Another method involves analyzing error messages and status codes returned by web servers.

These messages can provide clues about the server's configuration, software stack, and potential vulnerabilities.

Think of it as listening to someone's conversations to gather information about their interests and activities.

Furthermore, specialized tools and scripts are available for automated server-side technology fingerprinting.

These tools can send predefined requests to web servers, analyze responses, and generate reports containing detailed information about the server's characteristics.

Imagine it as having a digital detective on your team, tirelessly gathering information about web servers.

To illustrate the practicality of server-side technology fingerprinting, let's consider an example.

Imagine you are a cybersecurity analyst responsible for assessing the security of a client's website.

You decide to perform server-side technology fingerprinting to gather intelligence about the web server powering the site.

Using a tool like Nmap or Wappalyzer, you initiate scans and requests targeting the website's server.

Upon analyzing the HTTP response headers, you discover that the web server is Apache, version 2.4.41, running on a Linux operating system.

Additionally, you identify the presence of PHP, indicating that the website may be using server-side scripting.

With this information, you proceed to conduct further security assessments, searching for known vulnerabilities associated with Apache 2.4.41 and PHP.

You also assess the website's security configuration and conduct penetration testing to identify potential weaknesses.

By combining the insights from server-side technology fingerprinting with other security assessments, you provide your client with a comprehensive report outlining potential security risks and recommended mitigations.

In summary, server-side technology fingerprinting is a valuable technique in the digital world, allowing us to unveil the digital identities of web servers and the software powering them.

Much like detectives examining evidence to solve a case, we use this technique to gather intelligence, assess security, and investigate cyber incidents.

By understanding the server-side technologies in play, we enhance our ability to secure web environments, develop robust websites, and conduct effective cybersecurity assessments.

Chapter 4: Targeted Social Engineering

Let's embark on a journey into the intriguing world of spear phishing and email deception, where we unravel the art of targeted email-based attacks, exploring the tactics, motivations, and defenses that shape this digital landscape.

Imagine you receive an email that seems to come from your boss, urgently requesting sensitive financial information. You're inclined to trust it, but what if it's not really your boss?

This scenario illustrates the essence of spear phishing, a sophisticated form of cyberattack that leverages deception to exploit human vulnerabilities.

Spear phishing is not your typical email scam; it's a carefully crafted and highly targeted attack that aims to deceive a specific individual or organization.

Picture it as a skilled illusionist who knows your deepest fears and desires, crafting a performance designed to manipulate your perception.

The term "spear phishing" derives from the concept of using a spear rather than a net to catch fish. In the digital realm, it represents precision and focus, with attackers carefully selecting their targets.

Now, let's delve into the significance and implications of spear phishing in the ever-evolving landscape of cybersecurity.

Spear phishing attacks are highly effective because they prey on human psychology and trust.

Imagine it as a confidence trickster who gains your trust before swindling you.

In many cases, spear phishing emails appear to come from trusted sources, such as colleagues, superiors, or reputable organizations.

This impersonation is achieved through email spoofing, where attackers manipulate the sender's address and content to mimic someone the victim knows or trusts.

Think of it as a masterful impersonator assuming the identity of a loved one or authority figure.

The motivation behind spear phishing attacks can vary widely.

Some attackers seek financial gain, attempting to trick victims into transferring funds or disclosing sensitive financial information.

Others aim to steal intellectual property, trade secrets, or valuable data.

Imagine it as a digital heist targeting the crown jewels of a company or individual.

Certain spear phishing campaigns are politically motivated, intending to infiltrate government agencies or influence elections.

In these instances, attackers may impersonate political figures or organizations to deceive recipients.

Think of it as a covert operation with real-world consequences.

Moreover, spear phishing is not limited to individuals; organizations of all sizes are vulnerable.

Imagine it as a skilled burglar who can bypass a company's security systems by tricking an employee into granting access.

To carry out spear phishing attacks, cybercriminals conduct extensive research on their targets.

They gather information from various sources, such as social media, public records, and previous data breaches, to personalize their attacks.

Think of it as a private investigator who compiles a dossier on a target, enabling precise manipulation.

Now, let's explore the tactics and techniques employed by attackers in spear phishing campaigns.

One common tactic is pretexting, where attackers create a fabricated scenario or pretext to gain the victim's trust.

Imagine it as an actor who assumes a role to gain access to sensitive information.

Phishing emails often contain malicious attachments or links. When victims click on these links or open attachments, they may unknowingly download malware onto their devices.

Think of it as a Trojan horse, entering your digital fortress under the guise of a friendly gift.

In some cases, attackers use social engineering techniques to manipulate victims into taking specific actions, such as wire transfers or sharing login credentials.

Imagine it as a skilled persuader who convinces you to do something you wouldn't otherwise.

Another deceptive tactic is CEO fraud, where attackers impersonate high-ranking executives to request financial transactions or confidential information.

Think of it as an imposter who walks into a secure area using a stolen badge.

To defend against spear phishing attacks, organizations and individuals must adopt a multi-layered approach.

Imagine it as reinforcing the defenses of a castle to withstand a siege.

This approach includes employee training and awareness programs to educate individuals about the dangers of phishing and social engineering.

Think of it as teaching people to recognize a magician's tricks.

Email filtering and authentication mechanisms are crucial in identifying and blocking phishing emails.

Imagine it as having a security guard check the credentials of everyone entering a building.

Furthermore, implementing strong access controls, multi-factor authentication, and regular software patching can help reduce the attack surface for spear phishers.

Think of it as reinforcing the locks and gates of a fortress.

In addition, threat intelligence and monitoring can help organizations detect and respond to spear phishing attempts in real-time.

Imagine it as having a team of vigilant guards patrolling the castle walls.

To illustrate the practicality of spear phishing defenses, let's consider an example.

Imagine you work for a financial institution, and you receive an email that appears to come from your CEO.

The email requests that you transfer a substantial sum of money to a specific account urgently.

However, something about the email seems off to you.

Instead of immediately complying, you decide to verify the request.

You call your CEO using a known phone number, and he confirms that he never sent such an email.

Your suspicions were correct; it was a spear phishing attempt.

Thanks to your training and awareness, you prevented a potential financial loss and data breach.

In summary, spear phishing and email deception are sophisticated digital scams that exploit human psychology and trust.

Much like skilled illusionists, cybercriminals craft convincing narratives to manipulate their victims.

However, with awareness, education, and robust cybersecurity measures, individuals and organizations can defend against these deceptive tactics and protect their digital assets from harm.

Let's explore the intriguing world of impersonation and pretexting techniques, where we delve into the art of assuming false identities and creating convincing scenarios to deceive individuals and organizations.

Imagine a talented actor who can slip seamlessly into different roles, persuading others to believe in their authenticity.

Impersonation and pretexting are social engineering tactics that exploit human trust and empathy.

Think of them as theatrical performances where the actors are cybercriminals, and the stage is the digital realm.

To begin, let's demystify the concepts of impersonation and pretexting and understand why they matter in the realm of cybersecurity and social engineering.

Impersonation involves assuming the identity of someone else, whether it's a colleague, superior, or trusted entity.

Imagine it as a skilled mimic who can imitate voices, gestures, and mannerisms to perfection.

Pretexting, on the other hand, entails creating a fabricated scenario or pretext to gain a person's trust or cooperation.

Think of it as a storyteller weaving a tale so compelling that the listener becomes an active participant.

These techniques are not limited to cybercriminals; they are also used in legitimate contexts, such as undercover investigations, theatrical performances, or even role-playing games.

Now, let's explore the significance and applications of impersonation and pretexting in various domains.

In cybersecurity, these tactics are often employed to gain unauthorized access to systems, steal sensitive information, or manipulate individuals into revealing confidential data.

Imagine it as a digital infiltrator who assumes a trusted identity to breach digital fortresses.

Impersonation and pretexting are effective because they exploit human psychology.

Our innate inclination to trust others and our desire to help and cooperate can make us vulnerable to these tactics.

Think of it as a magician using misdirection to deceive their audience.

In the realm of corporate espionage, impersonation and pretexting can be used to infiltrate organizations, gather competitive intelligence, or compromise proprietary information.

Imagine it as a corporate spy who assumes a false identity to gain access to boardrooms and confidential meetings.

Moreover, these tactics are not limited to individuals; organizations can also fall victim to impersonation and pretexting.

Imagine it as an entire theater troupe working together to deceive a company's employees and gain access to sensitive data.

Now, let's delve into the practical aspects of impersonation and pretexting techniques.

One common method is email impersonation, where cybercriminals use email addresses that appear legitimate to deceive recipients.

Think of it as sending a message with a forged signature, convincing the recipient that it's from a trusted source.

Attackers can also impersonate trusted authorities, such as law enforcement officers, government officials, or company executives.

By assuming positions of authority, they can pressure victims into compliance or divulging sensitive information.

Imagine it as a con artist who claims to be an official, compelling you to follow their instructions.

In pretexting scenarios, attackers often create elaborate narratives to manipulate victims.

For example, they might pose as a tech support agent and claim that the victim's computer has a critical issue that requires immediate attention.

Think of it as a skilled storyteller crafting a tale that tugs at your emotions and convinces you to act.

Furthermore, pretexting can involve creating fake websites or landing pages that mimic legitimate ones.

Victims are then directed to these deceptive sites, where they may unknowingly enter sensitive information.

Imagine it as a forger creating a convincing replica of a masterpiece to deceive art collectors.

To defend against impersonation and pretexting, individuals and organizations must adopt a vigilant and cautious approach.

Imagine it as building strong defenses to protect against skillful impersonators and storytellers.

Employee training and awareness programs are essential to educate individuals about these tactics and how to recognize and respond to them.

Think of it as teaching people to spot the subtle cues that give away an impersonator's true identity.

Additionally, organizations can implement strict access controls, multi-factor authentication, and incident response plans to mitigate the risks associated with impersonation and pretexting.

Imagine it as reinforcing the security measures of a fortress to withstand a siege.

In summary, impersonation and pretexting are sophisticated social engineering tactics that exploit human psychology and trust.

Much like skilled actors and storytellers, cybercriminals use these techniques to assume false identities and create convincing scenarios.

However, with awareness, education, and robust cybersecurity measures, individuals and organizations can defend against these deceptive tactics and protect themselves from harm in the digital age.

Chapter 5: Advanced Network Scanning and Enumeration

Let's embark on a journey into the fascinating world of service version detection and banner grabbing, where we unravel the art of identifying and fingerprinting software and services running on networked systems, a crucial skill for cybersecurity professionals and ethical hackers alike.

Imagine you're a digital detective, investigating a mysterious building. You need to know what businesses are inside, but there are no signs. Instead, you listen for conversations and observe what each business is saying to its customers. This is similar to what service version detection and banner grabbing accomplish in the digital realm.

Service version detection and banner grabbing are reconnaissance techniques used to gather information about the software and services running on networked systems.

Think of them as the digital equivalent of peeking through windows to see what's happening inside a building.

Now, let's dive into the importance and applications of service version detection and banner grabbing in the field of cybersecurity.

These techniques are essential for identifying potential vulnerabilities in networked systems.

Imagine it as inspecting a building for weak points in its security.

By determining the software versions and configurations, security professionals can assess whether the systems are up to date with patches and updates.

Think of it as checking if a business has modern security measures in place.

Service version detection and banner grabbing are often the first steps in the process of vulnerability assessment and penetration testing.

Imagine it as a digital detective collecting clues before solving a case.

Furthermore, these techniques are crucial for ensuring compliance with security policies and regulations, especially in industries with strict requirements.

Think of it as an inspector verifying that a business adheres to safety standards.

Now, let's explore the practical aspects of service version detection and banner grabbing.

One common method involves sending specific requests to networked systems and analyzing the responses they provide.

Think of it as asking businesses in the building about their services, and noting down their responses.

The responses often include banners or headers that reveal information about the software and services, such as the product name, version number, and sometimes even the operating system.

Imagine it as businesses putting up signs with their names and services offered.

Specialized tools and scripts are available to automate the process of service version detection and banner grabbing.

These tools send predefined requests to target systems, capture the responses, and extract the relevant information.

Think of them as digital detectives with magnifying glasses, examining the fine print.

To illustrate the practicality of these techniques, let's consider an example.

Imagine you're a cybersecurity professional tasked with assessing the security of a company's web server.

You decide to start with service version detection and banner grabbing.

Using a tool like Nmap or Wireshark, you send requests to the web server and analyze the responses.

From the banners and headers in the responses, you discover that the server is running Apache HTTP Server version 2.4.41 and PHP version 7.3.19.

With this information, you can research whether any known vulnerabilities exist for these specific software versions.

You also check if the server's configuration adheres to best practices and security guidelines.

This initial reconnaissance helps you plan your next steps in securing the web server.

In summary, service version detection and banner grabbing are essential techniques for identifying and fingerprinting software and services on networked systems.

Much like detectives gathering information about businesses inside a building, these techniques provide valuable insights for cybersecurity professionals and ethical hackers.

By understanding the software and versions in play, security assessments can be more precise, vulnerabilities can be addressed, and networks can be better protected in the ever-evolving digital landscape.

Let's delve into the fascinating world of advanced enumeration techniques for Active Directory (AD) networks, where we explore the art of gathering detailed information about network resources, users, and configurations in a way that's vital for both attackers and defenders in the realm of cybersecurity.

Imagine you're an explorer, navigating a vast and complex digital terrain filled with hidden treasures and secrets. Advanced enumeration techniques are like your compass and map, guiding you to uncover valuable information.

Enumeration in an AD network is the process of listing and categorizing network resources, such as computers, users, groups, shares, and services.

Think of it as creating a comprehensive inventory of everything within a digital kingdom.

Now, let's delve into the importance and applications of advanced enumeration techniques in the context of Active Directory networks.

These techniques are essential for understanding the structure and layout of an AD network.

Imagine it as studying the architecture of a castle before attempting to infiltrate or defend it.

Enumeration helps security professionals identify potential vulnerabilities, misconfigurations, and weak points in the network.

Think of it as a vigilant guard discovering hidden entrances or weak spots in the castle's defenses.

Moreover, advanced enumeration is a crucial step in the process of penetration testing and ethical hacking.

Imagine it as a master thief who carefully maps out the castle's layout before attempting a heist.

Enumeration also plays a significant role in incident response and digital forensics.

Think of it as a detective gathering evidence to reconstruct the sequence of events in a crime.

Now, let's explore the practical aspects of advanced enumeration techniques for Active Directory networks.

One common technique is querying AD domain controllers using Lightweight Directory Access Protocol (LDAP).

This allows you to retrieve information about users, groups, computers, and other AD objects.

Imagine it as sending messengers to gather information from different parts of the kingdom.

LDAP queries can be tailored to extract specific information, such as all users in a particular group or computers with specific attributes.

Think of it as instructing your messengers to bring back only certain types of information.

Another technique involves using enumeration tools and scripts designed for AD networks.

These tools automate the process of querying AD and can provide detailed reports on network resources and configurations.

Imagine it as having skilled scouts who can explore and map the entire kingdom efficiently.

Additionally, enumeration can be performed using PowerShell, a powerful scripting language for Windows environments.

PowerShell scripts can query AD and extract information about users, groups, privileges, and more.

Think of it as having wizards who can magically gather information with the wave of a wand.

To illustrate the practicality of advanced enumeration techniques, let's consider an example.

Imagine you're a cybersecurity professional tasked with assessing the security of an organization's Active Directory network.

You start by using LDAP queries to retrieve information about users, groups, and computers in the domain.

With this information, you discover that there's a group named "Domain Admins" with several members who have extensive privileges.

You also find that some user accounts have weak passwords and are not subject to account lockout policies.

Using PowerShell scripts, you further enumerate the network, identifying shares with insecure permissions and potential misconfigurations.

With this comprehensive understanding of the network's structure and vulnerabilities, you can recommend security improvements and help protect the organization's digital assets.

In summary, advanced enumeration techniques are essential for gaining a deep understanding of Active Directory networks.

Much like explorers mapping out uncharted territories, these techniques provide valuable insights for cybersecurity professionals and ethical hackers.

By using enumeration to identify vulnerabilities and weaknesses, organizations can strengthen their defenses and ensure the security of their digital kingdoms in an ever-evolving cyber landscape.

Chapter 6: Anonymity and Privacy in Information Gathering

Let's dive into the fascinating world of maintaining anonymity through the use of Tor (The Onion Router) and Virtual Private Networks (VPNs), where we'll explore the art of concealing your online identity and activities in the digital realm.

Imagine you're donning a mask at a masquerade ball, where no one can discern your true identity. Tor and VPNs serve as your digital masks, allowing you to navigate the internet without revealing who you are.

Anonymity in the digital age is a concept that has become increasingly important, given the pervasive nature of online surveillance and data tracking.

Think of it as wearing sunglasses and a hat to blend into a crowd while keeping your true appearance hidden.

Now, let's delve into the significance and applications of Tor and VPNs in the realm of online anonymity and privacy.

Tor is a privacy-focused network that aims to conceal your online activities and location by routing your internet traffic through a series of volunteer-operated servers, encrypting it at each step.

Imagine it as a secret underground network of tunnels that obscure your digital footprints.

Tor is particularly valuable for individuals in regions with internet censorship, as it can help them access restricted content and communicate freely.

Think of it as a hidden passageway that allows you to bypass digital barriers and reach the information you seek.

VPNs, on the other hand, are secure tunnels that encrypt your internet traffic and route it through servers located in different geographic locations.

Imagine it as a private highway for your data, making it difficult for anyone to eavesdrop on your online activities.

VPNs are commonly used for various purposes, including protecting your data on public Wi-Fi networks, bypassing geo-restrictions on streaming content, and enhancing online security.

Think of it as a digital shield that guards your data and enables you to access online resources without geographical limitations.

Now, let's explore the practical aspects of using Tor and VPNs to maintain anonymity online.

Tor is accessible through the Tor Browser, a modified version of Mozilla Firefox that's designed to route your internet traffic through the Tor network.

Imagine it as a special browser that automatically connects you to the secret network of tunnels.

When you use the Tor Browser, your online activities, including web browsing and communication, are anonymized, as it's challenging for anyone to trace the traffic back to you.

Think of it as wearing a disguise while attending a masked ball, making it nearly impossible for others to identify you.

VPNs, on the other hand, require you to install a VPN client on your device and choose a server location from a list provided by your VPN service provider.

Imagine it as choosing a secret location to wear your digital mask from.

Once connected to a VPN server, your internet traffic is encrypted and routed through that server, making it appear as if your connection is originating from that location.

Think of it as teleporting your online presence to a different place while maintaining your anonymity.

Both Tor and VPNs can be used in tandem for enhanced privacy and anonymity. In this setup, your internet traffic first goes through the VPN, and then through the Tor network.

Imagine it as wearing multiple layers of masks and disguises, making it even more challenging for anyone to uncover your true identity.

To illustrate the practicality of Tor and VPNs in maintaining anonymity, let's consider an example.

Imagine you're a journalist in a country with strict censorship and surveillance laws. You need to access a blocked news website and communicate securely with sources.

You start by connecting to a VPN server located in a country with strong privacy laws. This not only encrypts your traffic but also makes it appear as if you're browsing from that country.

Next, you launch the Tor Browser, which further anonymizes your online activities. Now, you can access the blocked news website and communicate with sources without fear of being monitored or traced.

In summary, Tor and VPNs are powerful tools for maintaining anonymity and privacy in the digital age.

Much like wearing masks and disguises at a masquerade ball, these technologies allow you to conceal your online identity and activities while navigating the internet.

Whether you're bypassing censorship, protecting your data on public networks, or accessing geo-restricted content, Tor and VPNs serve as your digital masks and shields, ensuring your online presence remains private and secure.

Let's embark on a journey into the realm of secure communication channels and data protection, where we'll explore the art of safeguarding your digital conversations and sensitive information in today's interconnected and data-driven world.

Imagine you're having a private conversation in a soundproof room with walls made of unbreakable glass.

Secure communication channels and data protection serve as the digital equivalent, ensuring that your online conversations and data remain confidential and impervious to prying eyes.

In an age where digital communication is the norm, the importance of secure channels cannot be overstated.

Think of it as having a secure vault to store your most valuable possessions, making sure they are shielded from theft and unauthorized access.

Now, let's delve into the significance and applications of secure communication channels and data protection in the context of cybersecurity and personal privacy.

Secure communication channels are essential for protecting sensitive information, such as personal messages, financial transactions, and confidential business discussions.

Imagine it as sending your most private thoughts through an impenetrable tunnel, ensuring they reach their destination intact and secure.

Data protection, on the other hand, encompasses a broader scope, involving measures to safeguard data at rest, in transit, and during processing.

Think of it as a multi-layered fortress protecting your valuable digital assets from all angles.

Secure communication channels and data protection are vital for maintaining trust and confidentiality in various domains, including healthcare, finance, legal, and government sectors.

Imagine it as a trustworthy confidant who ensures that your most confidential matters are kept secret.

In healthcare, for instance, secure channels are crucial for transmitting patient records and sensitive medical information while adhering to strict privacy regulations like HIPAA.

Think of it as a secure envelope for sharing health-related information, preserving patients' privacy and well-being.

Moreover, secure communication channels play a pivotal role in e-commerce, ensuring that online transactions are encrypted and secure.

Imagine it as a protective shield around your financial details, preventing cybercriminals from intercepting and exploiting your sensitive data.

Now, let's explore the practical aspects of secure communication channels and data protection.

One common method for achieving secure communication is through the use of encryption protocols.

These protocols encode the information you send, making it unreadable to anyone without the decryption key.

Think of it as writing a message in a secret code that only the intended recipient can decipher.

HTTPS, for example, is a widely used encryption protocol that secures data transmission between web browsers and websites.

Imagine it as a secure letter sealed in an unbreakable envelope while being sent through a secure courier.

For email communication, PGP (Pretty Good Privacy) and S/MIME (Secure/Multipurpose Internet Mail Extensions) provide end-to-end encryption, ensuring that only the sender and recipient can read the email contents.

Think of it as sending a letter in a locked box, with only the recipient possessing the key to unlock it.

Additionally, secure communication channels are often established through the use of Virtual Private Networks (VPNs) and Secure Sockets Layer (SSL) technology.

VPNs encrypt your internet traffic and route it through secure servers, making it difficult for anyone to intercept or monitor your online activities.

Imagine it as traveling through a private tunnel while invisible to prying eyes.

SSL, on the other hand, is employed by websites to secure data transmission between your browser and the webserver.

Think of it as having a secure phone line when communicating with a trusted party.

Data protection involves not only securing data in transit but also safeguarding it when at rest.

Imagine it as a safe deposit box, ensuring that your valuable information remains protected even when not actively in use.

This is achieved through encryption of stored data, access controls, and robust authentication methods.

Think of it as storing your precious belongings in a fortified vault, with only authorized personnel granted access.

To illustrate the practicality of secure communication channels and data protection, let's consider an example.

Imagine you're an entrepreneur running an online store, and you need to process customer payments securely.

You implement HTTPS on your website to encrypt all payment transactions, ensuring that sensitive financial data is protected during the checkout process.

Additionally, you use a VPN to secure your connection to the e-commerce platform's backend, preventing unauthorized access to customer order details and payment information.

By taking these measures, you provide your customers with a safe and secure shopping experience, enhancing their trust and confidence in your online business.

In summary, secure communication channels and data protection are fundamental pillars of cybersecurity and personal privacy in our digital age.

Much like fortresses and safeguards that protect valuable treasures, these technologies ensure that your online conversations and sensitive information remain confidential and shielded from potential threats.

Whether it's safeguarding healthcare data, securing financial transactions, or protecting personal communications, the importance of secure communication channels and data protection cannot be overstated in today's interconnected world.

Chapter 7: Leveraging Automation and Scripting

Let's dive into the world of scripting languages for reconnaissance, where we'll explore the art of automating and streamlining the information-gathering process, making it faster and more efficient than ever before.

Imagine you have a team of tireless detectives at your disposal, each with a unique set of skills and abilities. Scripting languages serve as your digital detectives, executing predefined tasks to collect valuable data during the reconnaissance phase.

In the realm of cybersecurity and ethical hacking, reconnaissance is the initial step in assessing a target, and it involves gathering information about the target's systems, networks, and vulnerabilities.

Think of it as sending out your detectives to gather clues and intelligence before embarking on a mission.

Now, let's delve into the significance and applications of scripting languages in the context of reconnaissance.

Scripting languages play a vital role in automating repetitive tasks, such as scanning for open ports, identifying vulnerable services, and collecting information from websites.

Imagine it as having your detectives work tirelessly around the clock, saving you time and effort.

Efficiency is the name of the game in reconnaissance, and scripting languages offer a powerful toolset for achieving just that.

Think of it as having access to a treasure trove of tools that can quickly and accurately retrieve information.

These languages allow security professionals and ethical hackers to create custom scripts tailored to their specific reconnaissance needs.

Imagine it as giving your detectives the ability to specialize in gathering the exact information you require.

Moreover, scripting languages facilitate the integration of various reconnaissance tools and techniques into a cohesive workflow.

Think of it as equipping your detectives with advanced gadgets and tools, ensuring they work seamlessly together.

Python, Perl, Ruby, and Bash are some of the most commonly used scripting languages in reconnaissance.

Imagine it as having a team of seasoned detectives, each with their own unique skills and expertise.

Python, for instance, is renowned for its simplicity and versatility, making it an excellent choice for automating a wide range of reconnaissance tasks.

Think of it as having a detective who can adapt to any situation and solve complex puzzles.

Perl, on the other hand, is known for its powerful text-processing capabilities, making it ideal for parsing and extracting data from various sources.

Imagine it as a detective who excels in deciphering cryptic messages and extracting valuable information.

Ruby is prized for its elegant and concise syntax, making it a favorite among developers for writing clear and readable reconnaissance scripts.

Think of it as a detective who communicates fluently and efficiently with your team.

Bash, the default shell on most Unix-based systems, is handy for executing command-line tools and performing quick reconnaissance tasks.

Imagine it as your trusty detective who knows all the shortcuts and tricks of the trade.

Now, let's explore the practical aspects of using scripting languages for reconnaissance.

One common use case is web scraping, where scripts are employed to extract information from websites.

Imagine it as sending your detectives to search for specific clues and data on the vast landscape of the internet.

Python, with its rich ecosystem of web scraping libraries like BeautifulSoup and Scrapy, is a popular choice for this task.

Think of it as having a detective who specializes in sifting through web pages to find hidden gems of information.

Another common application is network scanning, where scripts are used to identify open ports, services, and potential vulnerabilities on target systems.

Imagine it as your detectives mapping out the layout of a building, noting all the entrances and potential weak points.

Nmap, a widely used open-source network scanner, can be scripted to automate these tasks, providing a comprehensive view of a target's network.

Think of it as equipping your detectives with advanced surveillance equipment to gather critical intelligence.

Moreover, scripting languages can be employed to automate reconnaissance tasks such as DNS enumeration, banner grabbing, and OS fingerprinting.

Imagine it as your detectives utilizing specialized tools to gather information about the target's infrastructure and software.

Python's versatility, for example, allows you to create custom scripts that leverage existing libraries and modules to perform these tasks efficiently.

Think of it as your detectives adapting to the specific needs of each mission.

To illustrate the practicality of scripting languages in reconnaissance, let's consider an example.

Imagine you're a cybersecurity professional tasked with assessing the security of a company's web application.

You decide to use Python to automate the reconnaissance process.

You write a script that utilizes the requests library to send HTTP requests to the target application, analyzing the responses for clues about the underlying technologies and potential vulnerabilities.

You also employ the Beautiful Soup library to parse HTML and extract valuable information from the website's source code.

With your Python script in hand, you're able to quickly and comprehensively gather data about the web application, allowing you to identify security weaknesses and recommend improvements.

In summary, scripting languages are indispensable tools for automating and enhancing reconnaissance efforts in the realm of cybersecurity and ethical hacking.

Much like having a team of skilled detectives, these languages empower professionals to automate tasks, extract valuable information, and streamline the reconnaissance process.

Whether it's web scraping, network scanning, or custom reconnaissance tasks, scripting languages provide the flexibility and power needed to gather crucial intelligence efficiently and effectively.

Let's embark on an exciting journey into the world of building automated information gathering tools, where we'll explore the art of creating custom solutions that streamline and enhance the reconnaissance process, making it more efficient and tailored to your specific needs.

Imagine having a toolkit that's not only versatile but also intuitive, capable of adapting to different scenarios and providing you with valuable insights effortlessly.

Automated information gathering tools serve as your digital assistants, tirelessly collecting data, and providing you with a comprehensive view of your target's digital landscape.

In the realm of cybersecurity and ethical hacking, reconnaissance is a critical phase that involves gathering information about a target's systems, networks, and vulnerabilities.

Think of it as sending out your trusted assistants to scout the terrain before embarking on a mission.

Now, let's delve into the significance and applications of building automated information gathering tools in the context of cybersecurity and digital investigations.

These tools play a pivotal role in automating repetitive and time-consuming reconnaissance tasks, such as scanning for open ports, identifying services, and collecting information from various sources.

Imagine it as having a team of dedicated assistants who can work tirelessly around the clock, saving you valuable time and effort.

Efficiency is a core aspect of reconnaissance, and building your automated tools can greatly enhance your efficiency and effectiveness.

Think of it as customizing your toolkit to ensure that it aligns perfectly with your unique needs and objectives.

Moreover, these tools empower security professionals and ethical hackers to tailor their reconnaissance efforts to specific targets and scenarios.

Imagine it as having the ability to train your assistants to excel in specific areas and tasks, ensuring that they meet your objectives precisely.

In addition to efficiency and customization, building your automated information gathering tools offers the advantage of adaptability.

Think of it as having a toolkit that evolves and grows with your needs and challenges, ensuring that you're always well-prepared.

To illustrate the practical aspects of building automated information gathering tools, let's explore some common use cases.

One of the most prevalent use cases is web scraping, where tools are created to extract information from websites automatically.

Imagine it as instructing your assistants to navigate the vast landscape of the internet, collecting data from websites efficiently and accurately.

Python, with its rich ecosystem of libraries like BeautifulSoup and Scrapy, is a popular choice for building web scraping tools.

Think of it as having a versatile and adaptable assistant who can decipher web pages, extract valuable information, and present it in a structured format.

Another common application is network scanning, where tools are designed to identify open ports, services, and potential vulnerabilities on target systems.

Imagine it as outfitting your assistants with advanced surveillance equipment, enabling them to map out the target's network and assess its security posture.

Nmap, an open-source network scanner, can be customized and automated to perform these tasks, providing you with a comprehensive view of the target's network.

Think of it as having a team of assistants equipped with specialized tools to gather critical intelligence.

Additionally, automated information gathering tools can be employed for tasks such as DNS enumeration, banner grabbing, and OS fingerprinting.

Imagine it as your assistants using specialized tools to gather information about the target's infrastructure and software, providing you with valuable insights.

Building these tools often involves using programming languages like Python, Ruby, or Bash, depending on your preferences and requirements.

Think of it as selecting the right assistant for the job, ensuring that they have the skills and expertise needed for the task at hand.

To further illustrate the practicality of building automated information gathering tools, let's consider an example.

Imagine you're a cybersecurity professional tasked with assessing the security of a company's network.

You decide to build a custom tool using Python that automates the reconnaissance process.

Your tool is designed to scan the network for open ports, identify active services, and perform banner grabbing to collect information about the software running on the target systems.

Additionally, you've programmed it to conduct OS fingerprinting to determine the operating systems used by the target hosts.

With your custom tool in action, you're able to quickly and comprehensively gather data about the company's network, allowing you to identify potential vulnerabilities and security weaknesses.

In summary, building automated information gathering tools is a valuable skill that can greatly enhance your capabilities in the realm of cybersecurity and ethical hacking.

Much like having a team of versatile and adaptable assistants, these tools empower you to automate tasks, collect valuable information, and streamline the reconnaissance process.

Whether it's web scraping, network scanning, or custom reconnaissance tasks, building your automated tools provides you with the flexibility and control needed to gather critical intelligence efficiently and effectively.

Chapter 8: Deceptive Reconnaissance Tactics

Let's delve into the intriguing world of honeypots and deception networks, where we'll explore the art of luring, deceiving, and ultimately outsmarting potential attackers in the ever-evolving landscape of cybersecurity.

Imagine having a digital trap, a virtual riddle that entices and bewilders adversaries, offering them a false sense of victory while you observe their every move.

Honeypots and deception networks serve as your strategic decoys, providing a layer of defense that not only detects threats but also diverts and confuses attackers, safeguarding your digital assets.

In the realm of cybersecurity, the concept of deception has been employed for centuries, often symbolized by the Trojan Horse, a cunning ploy used by the Greeks to infiltrate the city of Troy.

Think of it as setting up an elaborate illusion that lures adversaries into a carefully designed trap.

Now, let's delve into the significance and applications of honeypots and deception networks in the context of modern cybersecurity.

These techniques are crucial for early threat detection, providing security professionals with a proactive means to identify and respond to potential breaches.

Imagine it as having a network of sentinels and decoys that watch over your digital territory, alerting you to any suspicious activity.

Honeypots, in particular, are designed to mimic legitimate systems and services, acting as bait to attract malicious actors.

Think of it as placing a juicy piece of fruit amidst a field of thorns, tempting intruders to take the bait.

Deception networks, on the other hand, involve the strategic placement of deceptive elements within an organization's network, such as fake assets and false data.

Imagine it as creating a digital maze, complete with illusions and dead ends, that misleads and confounds potential attackers.

The primary goal of honeypots and deception networks is to divert and distract attackers from genuine assets, buying security teams valuable time to respond and mitigate threats.

Think of it as leading adversaries down a convoluted path, keeping them occupied while you reinforce your defenses.

Moreover, these techniques enable security professionals to gather valuable intelligence about adversaries' tactics, techniques, and motives.

Imagine it as studying the behavior of wildlife in the wilderness, observing their habits and patterns to better understand their actions.

Honeypots and deception networks provide insights into the evolving threat landscape, helping organizations adapt and fortify their defenses.

Think of it as having a telescope that allows you to peer into the world of cyber adversaries, gaining a deeper understanding of their strategies.

Now, let's explore the practical aspects of implementing honeypots and deception networks.

One common use case for honeypots involves setting up high-interaction honeypots that closely mimic production systems.

Imagine it as crafting a digital doppelganger of your critical assets, complete with vulnerabilities that lure attackers in.

These honeypots serve as a valuable early warning system, alerting security teams to suspicious activity and enabling them to respond swiftly.

Think of it as having a watchtower on the outskirts of your digital kingdom, providing a clear vantage point to spot incoming threats.

Low-interaction honeypots, on the other hand, simulate services with minimal functionality, making them less resource-intensive while still attracting attackers.

Imagine it as a cardboard cutout of a guard at a museum entrance, deceiving would-be thieves into thinking there's an actual sentinel on duty.

Deception networks extend beyond honeypots and encompass a broader strategy that includes fake assets, decoy credentials, and deceptive network traffic.

Think of it as building an intricate labyrinth within your network, filled with traps and mirages to confuse and deter intruders.

Additionally, honeypots and deception networks can be tailored to meet specific organizational needs, whether it's protecting critical infrastructure or gaining insights into specific threat actors.

Imagine it as customizing your defenses to fit the unique challenges and objectives of your organization.

To further illustrate the practicality of honeypots and deception networks, let's consider an example.

Imagine you're responsible for securing a financial institution's network, which is frequently targeted by cybercriminals seeking to steal sensitive customer data.

You decide to implement a high-interaction honeypot that mimics a database server containing valuable customer information.

This honeypot is equipped with realistic-looking credentials and data, making it an attractive target for attackers.

As soon as an intruder attempts to breach the honeypot, an alert is triggered, and security teams are notified of the breach.

While the attacker believes they've gained access to valuable data, they are actually within the confines of the honeypot, unable to cause any harm.

In the meantime, security teams analyze the attacker's tactics, learn about their motives, and adapt their defenses accordingly.

In summary, honeypots and deception networks are indispensable tools in the arsenal of modern cybersecurity.

Much like setting traps and creating illusions, these techniques provide organizations with a proactive means to detect and respond to threats while gathering valuable intelligence about adversaries.

Whether it's diverting and distracting attackers, studying their behavior, or customizing defenses, honeypots and deception networks play a crucial role in safeguarding digital assets in the ever-evolving world of cybersecurity.

Let's explore the intriguing world of misdirection and false flags in the realm of reconnaissance, where we'll uncover the art of veiling one's true intentions and identity, creating confusion, and strategically diverting attention to achieve specific objectives in the complex landscape of cybersecurity and ethical hacking.

Imagine a magician's sleight of hand, where the audience's attention is directed towards an illusion while the real magic happens elsewhere.

Misdirection and false flags serve as your digital smoke and mirrors, allowing you to manipulate perceptions and deceive potential adversaries.

In the realm of cybersecurity and ethical hacking, these techniques are akin to strategic maneuvers on a digital battlefield, where the element of surprise and confusion can tip the scales in your favor.

Think of it as donning a cloak of invisibility, concealing your true intentions while you navigate the intricate web of digital interactions.

Now, let's delve into the significance and applications of misdirection and false flags in the context of reconnaissance. These techniques are essential for achieving strategic objectives, whether it's concealing your identity, diverting attention away from critical assets, or leading adversaries down a carefully constructed path.

Imagine it as orchestrating a complex dance of shadows and illusions, where every move is calculated to achieve a specific outcome.

One primary application of misdirection is obscuring the true source of an attack or operation, making it appear as if it originates from a different entity or location.

Think of it as wearing a mask, assuming a different persona to cloak your true identity and motives.

False flags, on the other hand, involve planting digital breadcrumbs that intentionally mislead investigators and adversaries.

Imagine it as creating a breadcrumb trail that leads in the wrong direction, confounding anyone who attempts to trace your steps.

The primary goal of misdirection and false flags is to create ambiguity, making it difficult for adversaries to discern your true intentions and objectives.

Think of it as leaving a trail of digital footprints that lead to dead ends and false conclusions, leaving them puzzled and uncertain.

Moreover, misdirection and false flags can be employed to protect critical assets and infrastructure from targeted attacks.

Imagine it as building an intricate maze around your digital fortress, with multiple entry points and false pathways that bewilder potential intruders.

These techniques serve as a strategic layer of defense, ensuring that attackers are not only deterred but also led astray if they attempt to breach your defenses.

Think of it as constructing a castle with hidden passages and secret doors, where every path leads to a different outcome.

Now, let's explore the practical aspects of implementing misdirection and false flags.

One common use case for misdirection is the manipulation of DNS records, where attackers alter DNS settings to redirect traffic to a decoy server or a false IP address.

Imagine it as changing road signs to lead travelers away from their intended destination, diverting them to a different route.

By doing so, attackers can effectively hide their true infrastructure and intentions while leading investigators and security teams down the wrong path.

Think of it as creating a maze of digital signposts that point in every direction except the correct one.

False flags, on the other hand, involve leaving behind digital artifacts that attribute an attack or operation to a different entity or nation-state.

Imagine it as planting a flag with a foreign emblem at a crime scene, creating the illusion of a different perpetrator.

These artifacts can include altered timestamps, language patterns, and other elements that mislead investigators and deflect suspicion.

Think of it as crafting a narrative that points towards a fictional antagonist, diverting attention from the true orchestrator of the operation.

To further illustrate the practicality of misdirection and false flags, let's consider an example.

Imagine you're a cybersecurity professional tasked with defending a high-value target, such as a critical infrastructure facility.

You decide to implement misdirection and false flags as part of your defensive strategy.

You configure the network's DNS settings to redirect traffic away from the actual servers and towards a decoy network segment.

This decoy network segment contains dummy servers and services designed to mimic the real infrastructure.

As attackers attempt to breach the network, they are led into the decoy segment, where their activities are closely monitored.

Meanwhile, you leave behind false artifacts, such as altered log entries and fabricated digital fingerprints, pointing to a fictitious adversary.

The combination of misdirection and false flags not only thwarts the attackers but also confuses and misleads them, making it challenging for them to discern the true nature of the network.

In summary, misdirection and false flags are powerful tools in the arsenal of cybersecurity and ethical hacking.

Much like a magician's trickery, these techniques allow you to manipulate perceptions, hide your true intentions, and strategically divert attention to achieve specific objectives.

Whether it's obscuring your identity, leading adversaries astray, or protecting critical assets, misdirection and false flags play a crucial role in the complex and ever-evolving landscape of cybersecurity.

Chapter 9: Vulnerability Scanning and Assessment

Let's embark on a fascinating journey into the world of advanced vulnerability scanning tools, where we'll uncover the cutting-edge technologies and strategies that empower cybersecurity professionals and ethical hackers to identify and mitigate vulnerabilities in the intricate landscape of digital systems and networks.

Imagine having a specialized toolkit, an arsenal of digital detectives armed with state-of-the-art gadgets, tirelessly scanning the digital terrain for weaknesses and vulnerabilities.

Advanced vulnerability scanning tools serve as your vigilant guardians, continuously monitoring your digital assets, and alerting you to potential threats.

In the realm of cybersecurity, these tools are akin to having a team of expert investigators who tirelessly search for hidden vulnerabilities that could be exploited by adversaries.

Think of it as deploying a battalion of sentinels who constantly patrol the digital frontier, ensuring the safety and integrity of your systems.

Now, let's delve into the significance and applications of advanced vulnerability scanning tools in the context of modern cybersecurity.

These tools are instrumental in proactively identifying vulnerabilities in software, networks, and systems before malicious actors can exploit them.

Imagine it as having a team of cyber detectives who investigate every nook and cranny of your digital environment, uncovering potential weak points and security holes.

Vulnerability scanning tools provide organizations with a vital line of defense, enabling them to patch and secure vulnerabilities before they can be leveraged for attacks.

Think of it as having an early warning system that detects potential threats and allows you to take preemptive action.

One of the primary applications of advanced vulnerability scanning tools is automated vulnerability assessment.

Imagine it as conducting a comprehensive health check of your digital infrastructure, where every component is examined for potential weaknesses.

These tools scan networks, systems, and applications to identify vulnerabilities, misconfigurations, and weaknesses in security controls.

Think of it as a regular medical checkup for your digital assets, ensuring they remain robust and resilient.

Moreover, advanced vulnerability scanning tools are essential for compliance and risk management.

Imagine it as having a regulatory compliance officer who ensures that your digital environment meets industry standards and adheres to security best practices.

These tools help organizations assess their security posture, identify vulnerabilities that could lead to data breaches or compliance violations, and prioritize remediation efforts.

Think of it as a risk management tool that helps you make informed decisions to protect your organization's reputation and assets.

Now, let's explore the practical aspects of implementing advanced vulnerability scanning tools.

One common use case involves network vulnerability scanning, where tools are deployed to identify vulnerabilities in network devices, such as routers, switches, and firewalls.

Imagine it as sending a team of investigators to inspect every lock and key in your digital fortress, ensuring that no entrance is left unguarded.

These tools perform scans to detect open ports, services, and potential vulnerabilities, allowing organizations to address security weaknesses promptly.

Think of it as having a security audit of your network infrastructure, providing insights into potential entry points for attackers.

Another crucial application is web application vulnerability scanning.

Imagine it as having a squad of experts who meticulously examine every nook and cranny of your web applications, searching for vulnerabilities that could be exploited by attackers.

These tools assess web applications for common vulnerabilities such as SQL injection, cross-site scripting (XSS), and insecure authentication mechanisms.

Think of it as having a team of ethical hackers who scrutinize your web applications, ensuring they are fortified against potential threats.

Furthermore, advanced vulnerability scanning tools can be utilized for host-based vulnerability assessment.

Imagine it as inspecting the foundation and structure of your digital properties, making sure that every component is solid and secure.

These tools scan individual hosts, such as servers and endpoints, to identify vulnerabilities in the operating system, installed software, and configurations.

Think of it as having a home inspector who checks every room and corner for potential hazards.

To further illustrate the practicality of advanced vulnerability scanning tools, let's consider an example.

Imagine you're the head of cybersecurity for a financial institution, responsible for protecting sensitive customer data and financial assets.

You decide to implement advanced vulnerability scanning tools as part of your security strategy.

You deploy network vulnerability scanning tools to regularly assess your network infrastructure, identifying potential weaknesses in routers, switches, and firewalls.

Additionally, you use web application vulnerability scanning tools to evaluate your online banking platform, ensuring that it's impervious to attacks like SQL injection and XSS.

Furthermore, host-based vulnerability assessment tools are employed to scan servers and endpoints, ensuring that the operating systems and software are up-to-date and secure.

With these tools in place, your cybersecurity team is equipped to proactively identify and remediate vulnerabilities, safeguarding the financial institution's digital assets and maintaining the trust of its customers.

In summary, advanced vulnerability scanning tools are indispensable in the world of cybersecurity and ethical hacking.

Much like having a team of expert investigators, these tools continuously monitor digital environments, uncover vulnerabilities, and empower organizations to take preemptive action.

Whether it's assessing network security, fortifying web applications, or inspecting host configurations, advanced vulnerability scanning tools play a pivotal role in maintaining the resilience and integrity of digital systems and networks in today's dynamic and evolving threat landscape.

Let's embark on a captivating journey into the world of vulnerability exploitation and post-exploitation techniques, where we'll uncover the intricate strategies and methods employed by ethical hackers and security professionals to leverage vulnerabilities and gain control over digital systems and networks.

Imagine vulnerability exploitation as a key that opens a door into a secure fortress, allowing access to its inner chambers.

In the realm of cybersecurity, this process involves identifying weaknesses and utilizing them to breach a system's defenses.

Think of it as a chess match, where each move is calculated to exploit a vulnerability and gain a strategic advantage.

Vulnerability exploitation is a critical skill in the arsenal of ethical hackers, enabling them to simulate real-world attacks and help organizations fortify their defenses.

Now, let's delve into the significance and applications of vulnerability exploitation and post-exploitation techniques in the context of modern cybersecurity.

These techniques play a crucial role in assessing an organization's security posture, allowing ethical hackers to identify weaknesses and vulnerabilities before malicious actors can exploit them.

Imagine it as a simulated assault on a fortress, where defenders learn from the attack and reinforce their defenses.

Vulnerability exploitation is not about causing harm but rather about uncovering weaknesses and helping organizations strengthen their security.

Think of it as a stress test for digital systems, revealing areas that need improvement.

One primary application of vulnerability exploitation is penetration testing, where ethical hackers mimic real-world attacks to evaluate an organization's defenses.

Imagine it as a controlled battle, where ethical hackers and defenders engage in a strategic contest to identify vulnerabilities and fortify security.

These tests assess a system's resilience, helping organizations understand their vulnerabilities and prioritize remediation efforts.

Think of it as a simulated war game, where the goal is to uncover weaknesses before real adversaries can exploit them.

Moreover, vulnerability exploitation and post-exploitation techniques are essential for understanding the impact of potential security breaches.

Imagine it as investigating a crime scene, where forensic experts analyze evidence to reconstruct the sequence of events.

These techniques allow ethical hackers and security professionals to assess the extent of a breach, determine what data or systems may have been compromised, and take steps to contain and mitigate the damage.

Think of it as a digital detective's toolkit, helping experts piece together the puzzle of a security incident.

Now, let's explore the practical aspects of vulnerability exploitation and post-exploitation techniques.

One common method of vulnerability exploitation is the use of exploit code, which takes advantage of specific vulnerabilities to gain unauthorized access to a system or application.

Imagine it as finding a secret passage into a fortress, where the exploit code is the key that opens the door.

These codes are designed to trigger vulnerabilities and execute malicious actions, such as gaining administrative privileges or stealing sensitive data.

Think of it as a lockpicker's tool, allowing ethical hackers to test a system's security by attempting to breach it.

Additionally, post-exploitation techniques come into play after an attacker gains access to a system.

Imagine it as infiltrating an enemy's fortress and then navigating its inner chambers to achieve specific objectives.

These techniques involve maintaining access, escalating privileges, and exfiltrating data while evading detection.

Think of it as a spy's mission, where the goal is to gather intelligence or accomplish a specific mission within the compromised system.

To further illustrate the practicality of vulnerability exploitation and post-exploitation techniques, let's consider an example.

Imagine you're an ethical hacker hired by a financial institution to assess the security of its online banking platform.

Your goal is to identify vulnerabilities that could be exploited by malicious actors to compromise customer accounts or steal sensitive financial data.

You begin by conducting penetration testing, using exploit code to target known vulnerabilities in the web application.

Imagine it as attempting to breach the fortress of the online banking platform by exploiting weaknesses in its defenses.

Once you successfully exploit a vulnerability, you gain access to the application and initiate post-exploitation techniques.

Think of it as infiltrating the fortress and then navigating its inner chambers to achieve specific objectives.

You escalate your privileges to gain control over the application's database, where customer account information is stored.

This is akin to acquiring the keys to the vault within the fortress.

You then exfiltrate a sample of customer data, demonstrating the potential impact of a real-world attack.

Think of it as a reconnaissance mission within the compromised system, gathering intelligence to assess the extent of the breach.

After completing your assessment, you provide the financial institution with a comprehensive report detailing the vulnerabilities you discovered and the potential consequences of exploitation.

Think of it as a battle plan, outlining the weaknesses that need to be fortified to protect against real adversaries.

In summary, vulnerability exploitation and post-exploitation techniques are essential elements of modern cybersecurity and ethical hacking.

Much like a skilled locksmith, ethical hackers use these techniques to test and strengthen the security of digital systems and networks.

Whether it's simulating attacks, investigating security incidents, or helping organizations fortify their defenses, vulnerability exploitation and post-exploitation techniques play a vital role in safeguarding the digital realm in an ever-evolving threat landscape.

Chapter 10: Legal and Ethical Aspects of Advanced Information Gathering

Let's explore the intricate world of privacy laws and compliance, where the protection of personal information and data privacy are at the forefront of modern society's concerns. Imagine privacy laws as the guardians of our digital lives, setting the rules to safeguard our personal information in an increasingly interconnected world.

In today's digital age, our personal data is more valuable than ever, and it's crucial to have a robust framework in place to ensure that it's handled responsibly and ethically. Think of privacy laws as the rules of the game, guiding organizations and individuals on how personal data should be collected, processed, and protected.

Privacy laws and compliance are not just about legal obligations; they are also about respecting the fundamental rights of individuals. Imagine it as a social contract, where we agree to protect each other's privacy in exchange for the benefits of a connected world.

One of the most significant privacy laws globally is the General Data Protection Regulation (GDPR), enacted by the European Union. Think of GDPR as a gold standard for data protection, setting strict requirements for organizations that process personal data, regardless of where they are located.

GDPR emphasizes transparency, consent, and the rights of individuals over their data. It's a game-changer in the world of privacy laws, forcing organizations to rethink their data handling practices and prioritize the privacy of their customers.

But GDPR is not alone; there are many other privacy laws and regulations worldwide, each with its own set of requirements and nuances. Think of them as pieces of a global puzzle, coming together to form a comprehensive framework for data protection.

In the United States, for example, the California Consumer Privacy Act (CCPA) has gained prominence, giving Californians more control over their personal data. It's a reflection of the growing demand for data privacy rights in the digital age.

Imagine privacy laws as a safety net, providing individuals with the assurance that their personal data will not be misused or mishandled. These laws also empower individuals with rights such as the right to access their data, the right to be forgotten, and the right to data portability.

Privacy compliance is not just a legal requirement; it's also a business imperative. Organizations that fail to comply with privacy laws risk not only legal consequences but also damage to their reputation and trustworthiness. Think of it as a competitive advantage, where customers are more likely to trust and engage with businesses that prioritize their privacy.

Moreover, privacy laws are not static; they evolve to address new challenges and technologies. Think of them as living documents, adapting to the changing landscape of data privacy.

For example, as artificial intelligence and machine learning become more prevalent, privacy laws may need to incorporate provisions to protect against automated decision-making based on personal data. Imagine it as a constantly updating rulebook for the digital age.

Privacy compliance is a multidisciplinary effort, involving legal experts, IT professionals, data analysts, and privacy officers. Think of it as a collaborative endeavor, where different stakeholders work together to ensure that personal data is handled in a compliant and ethical manner.

Privacy impact assessments are one of the tools organizations use to assess the impact of their data processing activities on individuals' privacy. Imagine it as a risk assessment, helping organizations identify and mitigate potential privacy risks.

Privacy laws also require organizations to appoint a Data Protection Officer (DPO) in some cases. Think of the DPO as a privacy guardian within the organization, responsible for ensuring compliance with privacy laws and acting as a point of contact for individuals and authorities.

Privacy compliance is not just a matter of checking boxes; it's about embedding a culture of privacy within an organization. Think of it as a mindset, where every employee understands the importance of protecting personal data and takes it seriously.

Data breaches are a significant concern in the world of privacy, and many privacy laws require organizations to report breaches promptly. Think of it as a safety alarm, alerting individuals and authorities when their data may have been compromised.

Privacy laws also establish penalties for non-compliance, which can be substantial. Imagine it as a deterrent, discouraging organizations from neglecting their privacy responsibilities.

In the digital age, data is a currency, and privacy laws are the vaults that protect it. Think of them as safeguards, ensuring that personal data remains in trusted hands.

Privacy compliance is not an option; it's a necessity in today's data-driven world. Think of it as a responsibility, where organizations and individuals share the duty of preserving the privacy and integrity of personal data.

In summary, privacy laws and compliance are at the heart of data protection in the digital age. They are the rules that govern how personal data should be handled, and they play a crucial role in safeguarding individual rights and trust in the digital world. Imagine them as the guardians of our digital lives, ensuring that our personal information remains secure and respected.

Let's delve into the crucial topic of reporting vulnerabilities responsibly and ethically, a fundamental aspect of the ethical hacking and cybersecurity community that plays a pivotal role in maintaining the security of digital systems and protecting sensitive data.

Imagine yourself as a digital detective, uncovering vulnerabilities that could potentially compromise the security of a company's information systems.

In this role, you're not a cybercriminal seeking to exploit weaknesses; instead, you're a cybersecurity professional committed to strengthening defenses.

Think of responsible vulnerability reporting as the ethical obligation that comes with your expertise—a responsibility to act as a guardian of digital security.

Vulnerabilities are like hidden cracks in the armor of digital systems, and they can be discovered by diligent security researchers, ethical hackers, or even vigilant users.

These vulnerabilities, if left unchecked, can be exploited by malicious actors to breach systems, steal data, or cause havoc.

Imagine them as security holes in a fortress that need to be patched before they can be exploited by intruders.

Responsible reporting begins with the discovery of a vulnerability, whether it's through manual testing, automated scans, or user reports.

Once identified, the next step is to verify the vulnerability's existence and potential impact.

Think of this phase as confirming that the crack in the fortress wall is real and that it could indeed be exploited.

Once you've confirmed the vulnerability, it's essential to gather all the necessary information, including details about the affected system, the potential impact of the vulnerability, and any proof of concept that demonstrates its exploitability.

Imagine this phase as collecting evidence to support your case, much like a detective gathering clues at a crime scene.

With all the information in hand, it's time to establish clear communication with the organization or entity responsible for the vulnerable system.

Think of this as reaching out to the fortress owner and informing them about the crack in their defenses.

Responsible reporting should be conducted through appropriate channels, such as a designated security contact, a bug bounty program, or a support portal.

This ensures that the information reaches the right people who can take action.

Imagine it as reporting a security breach to the castle's authorities so that they can reinforce their defenses.

When reporting a vulnerability, it's crucial to provide a clear and detailed description of the issue, along with step-by-step instructions on how to reproduce it.

Think of this as providing the castle's owner with a comprehensive report on where the crack is located and how it can be exploited.

Responsible reporting also includes setting a reasonable disclosure timeline. This timeline should allow the organization ample time to assess and address the vulnerability.

Imagine it as giving the castle's owner a reasonable period to repair the crack in their defenses before it's made public.

Responsible disclosure typically follows a coordinated process between the reporter and the organization. This collaborative approach ensures that fixes are in place before the vulnerability is disclosed to the public.

Think of this process as a joint effort between the castle's owner and the security researcher to seal the crack in the fortress wall.

In some cases, organizations may offer bug bounties or rewards for responsibly reported vulnerabilities.

Imagine this as a token of appreciation, where the castle's owner rewards you for helping them fortify their defenses.

Responsible reporting is not just a moral obligation but also a legal one in many jurisdictions. Failure to report vulnerabilities responsibly can have legal consequences.

Think of it as following the law and ethical guidelines to ensure that your actions contribute to the greater good of digital security.

When vulnerabilities are reported responsibly, organizations can take prompt action to patch their systems, preventing potential breaches and data leaks.

Imagine it as the castle's owner quickly repairing the crack in the fortress wall, making it impervious to intruders.

Responsible reporting also helps maintain trust between security researchers, ethical hackers, and organizations. When organizations see the value in responsible disclosure, they are more likely to collaborate with the security community.

Think of it as building a strong partnership between those who protect digital fortresses and those who own them.

While responsible reporting is crucial, it's also essential to be prepared for various scenarios. Sometimes, organizations may not respond promptly or may even ignore vulnerability reports.

Imagine this as encountering a castle owner who is slow to respond or dismissive of the security concern.

In such cases, it's crucial to exercise patience and persistence. You can escalate the issue through legal channels or involve the cybersecurity community.

Think of it as seeking help from the authorities or enlisting the support of fellow security experts to address the vulnerability.

Responsible reporting extends beyond simply identifying and disclosing vulnerabilities. It also involves a commitment to responsible and ethical behavior within the security community.

Imagine it as being a good digital citizen, promoting a culture of integrity, honesty, and collaboration among security professionals.

In summary, responsible reporting of vulnerabilities is a cornerstone of ethical hacking and cybersecurity.

Think of it as an essential duty, akin to being a digital guardian, where your actions contribute to the overall security and trustworthiness of the digital realm.

By responsibly reporting vulnerabilities, you help fortify the defenses of digital systems, protect sensitive data, and foster a culture of responsible and ethical behavior in the cybersecurity community.

BOOK 3
THE ETHICAL HACKER'S FIELD GUIDE TO TARGET DATA
ACQUISITION

ROB BOTWRIGHT

Chapter 1: Understanding Target Data Acquisition

Let's embark on the journey of defining data acquisition objectives, a crucial step in the process of collecting information and insights that will shape your decisions and actions. Imagine data acquisition objectives as the guiding stars that help navigate the vast sea of data available in today's digital landscape.

In the vast realm of data, clarity of purpose is essential, and that's where defining objectives comes into play.

Think of data acquisition objectives as your destination on a treasure hunt, setting a clear path to uncover valuable insights or information.

Before diving into the process, it's vital to ask yourself what specific goals or outcomes you aim to achieve through data acquisition.

Imagine this as charting your course on a map, marking the places you want to explore and the treasures you hope to uncover.

Start by considering the context of your data acquisition efforts. Are you a business seeking to better understand customer preferences, a researcher exploring scientific phenomena, or a government agency looking to enhance public services?

Think of this as understanding the purpose behind your journey—knowing why you're setting sail in the first place.

Once you've established the context, it's time to define your objectives with precision.

Imagine your objectives as the compass that will guide you through the data landscape, ensuring you stay on course.

Are you aiming to gain insights into consumer behavior, improve operational efficiency, identify potential risks, or simply satisfy your curiosity?

Think of these objectives as the specific destinations on your data journey—clearly defined and attainable.

It's essential to make your objectives SMART: Specific, Measurable, Achievable, Relevant, and Time-bound.

Specific objectives narrow down your focus, ensuring you know exactly what you're looking for.

Think of them as the coordinates on your map, pinpointing the exact locations of your data treasures.

Measurable objectives allow you to track progress and success.

Imagine them as mile markers along your journey, showing how far you've come and how much further you need to go.

Achievable objectives are realistic and within your reach.

Think of them as setting achievable goals during your voyage—ones that you can realistically strive for.

Relevant objectives align with your overall purpose and mission.

Imagine them as destinations that are not only interesting but also relevant to your journey's purpose.

Time-bound objectives come with deadlines, keeping you on track and preventing aimless wandering.

Think of them as setting a timeline for your journey, ensuring you reach your destinations in a timely manner.

Let's consider an example: Suppose you're a marketing manager for an e-commerce company, and your objective is to improve customer engagement through targeted email campaigns.

Imagine this as your specific destination—enhancing customer engagement through email campaigns.

Measurable objectives could include achieving a 10% increase in email open rates and a 15% increase in click-through rates.

Think of these as the metrics that will indicate your progress and success.

Achievable objectives might involve optimizing email content and segmenting the customer base effectively.

Imagine these as realistic steps you can take to reach your destination.

Relevant objectives could focus on aligning email campaigns with customer preferences and behaviors.

Think of them as ensuring that your efforts are not only effective but also meaningful to your audience.

Time-bound objectives could involve implementing changes within the next quarter and evaluating results within six months.

Imagine this as the timeline for your journey, keeping you on track and accountable.

Defining data acquisition objectives is not a one-time process. It's a dynamic and iterative practice.

Think of it as regularly checking your compass to ensure you're heading in the right direction.

As you progress, you may refine your objectives based on new insights and changing circumstances.

Imagine this as adjusting your course to stay aligned with your ultimate goals.

Data acquisition is a valuable tool for achieving objectives, but it's essential to strike a balance between quantity and quality.

Think of data as a resource that needs to be managed effectively to achieve your goals.

Collecting vast amounts of data without a clear purpose can lead to overwhelming and unmanageable datasets.

Imagine it as trying to navigate a dense forest without a map—easy to get lost and disoriented.

On the other hand, focusing on data that directly supports your objectives ensures a more targeted and effective approach.

Think of this as using a GPS that guides you directly to your desired destinations.

Consider data sources that are relevant to your objectives, whether they are internal databases, customer feedback, social media interactions, or external market research.

Imagine these data sources as the tools and instruments you need for your journey.

Ensure that data acquisition methods align with your objectives.

Think of this as choosing the right vehicles for your exploration—whether it's surveys, analytics tools, sensors, or data scraping techniques.

Data acquisition should also consider data quality and integrity.

Imagine data quality as the condition of the roads you travel on—smooth and reliable routes that lead to accurate insights.

Data integrity ensures that the information you collect is trustworthy and free from errors.

Think of it as ensuring that the maps and guides you rely on are accurate and up-to-date.

It's crucial to stay mindful of data privacy and ethical considerations throughout the acquisition process.

Think of data privacy as respecting the boundaries and permissions of the territories you explore.

Adhering to ethical guidelines ensures that your data acquisition practices are responsible and fair.

Imagine it as being a conscientious traveler, respecting the local customs and cultures of the places you visit.

As you progress in your data acquisition journey, continuously evaluate your progress and adjust your approach as needed.

Think of this as regularly checking your compass and making course corrections to ensure you stay on the right track.

In summary, defining data acquisition objectives is a critical step in any data-driven journey.

Imagine it as setting clear destinations and charting a course to reach them.

With SMART objectives, a focus on data quality, and ethical considerations, you'll navigate the data landscape effectively, uncover valuable insights, and achieve your goals.

Let's explore the world of data acquisition planning and strategy—a fundamental aspect of any data-driven endeavor that can spell the difference between success and confusion.

Think of data acquisition planning as the blueprint for your data journey, helping you navigate the complex landscape of information with purpose and direction.

In the age of data abundance, the ability to acquire, manage, and leverage data effectively has become a competitive advantage.

Imagine data acquisition planning as the compass that guides you through this vast and sometimes turbulent sea of information.

At its core, data acquisition planning involves outlining a systematic approach to collect, process, and utilize data to achieve specific goals and objectives.

Think of it as charting your course on a treasure hunt— identifying the treasures you seek and planning the steps to uncover them.

Before embarking on any data acquisition endeavor, it's crucial to define your objectives clearly.

Imagine these objectives as the North Star of your journey, providing a sense of direction and purpose.

What do you aim to achieve with the data you collect? Are you looking to improve customer satisfaction, optimize operations, or enhance decision-making?

Think of these objectives as the destinations on your data journey, each with a unique set of challenges and opportunities.

Once you have a clear sense of your objectives, it's time to consider the scope of your data acquisition efforts.

Think of scope as the boundaries that define the extent of your data journey.

Are you focusing on a specific department within your organization, a particular dataset, or a broader data ecosystem that includes external sources?

Imagine this as choosing the territory you want to explore on your treasure hunt.

With objectives and scope in mind, it's essential to identify the data sources that will fuel your journey.

Think of data sources as the springs and wells that provide the water for your expedition.

These sources could be internal, such as your organization's databases, customer feedback, or sensor data, or external, like market research, social media, or public datasets.

Consider the quality of these data sources, ensuring that they are reliable, accurate, and relevant to your objectives.

Imagine data quality as the purity of the water you collect— clean and trustworthy.

Data acquisition planning also involves determining the frequency and timing of data collection.

Think of this as setting up regular watering holes along your journey to ensure a consistent supply of information.

Will you collect data in real-time, daily, weekly, or on a seasonal basis?

Consider the rhythm that aligns with your objectives and the nature of the data you're gathering.

In addition to frequency, think about the methods and tools you'll use for data acquisition.

Imagine these methods and tools as the instruments you bring on your expedition.

Will you rely on surveys, web scraping, sensors, or analytics platforms to gather data?

Choose the ones that best suit your objectives and the nature of the data sources.

Data acquisition planning should also address data security and privacy.

Think of data security as the protective gear you wear on your journey to safeguard your findings.

Ensure that you have measures in place to protect sensitive information and comply with relevant regulations.

Privacy considerations are like respecting the boundaries and customs of the lands you explore.

Respect the privacy rights of individuals whose data you collect, and be transparent about your data handling practices.

As you plan your data acquisition strategy, consider the scalability of your approach.

Think of scalability as the ability to adapt and expand your journey as needed.

Can your strategy accommodate growth, increased data volumes, and evolving objectives?

Ensure that your approach is flexible and can accommodate changes and new discoveries along the way.

Communication and collaboration are essential components of data acquisition planning.

Think of these as the fellow travelers who join you on your journey.

Establish clear lines of communication within your organization, ensuring that relevant stakeholders are informed and involved.

Collaborate with experts and teams who can provide valuable insights and expertise.

A data acquisition plan should also outline data processing and analysis methods.

Think of data processing as the way you refine and purify the treasures you uncover.

Will you use data cleansing, transformation, or enrichment techniques?

Consider how you'll prepare the data for analysis and derive meaningful insights.

Data analysis is like turning those treasures into valuable gems.

What tools and methods will you employ to extract actionable insights and make informed decisions?

Consider the skills and resources needed to carry out the analysis effectively.

Ensure that you have a clear plan for interpreting the results and translating them into actionable strategies.

Think of this as polishing the gems you've discovered, making them shine and ready for use.

Data visualization is an essential aspect of data acquisition planning.

Think of data visualization as the art of displaying your gems in a way that's easy to understand and appreciate.

Choose visualization techniques that resonate with your audience and convey insights effectively.

Consider the use of charts, graphs, dashboards, and reports to communicate your findings.

Data acquisition planning should also address data storage and management.

Imagine data storage as the vault where you safeguard your precious treasures.

Choose storage solutions that align with the volume and nature of the data you collect.

Consider scalability, security, and accessibility when selecting storage options.

Ensure that you have a data management strategy in place, including data retention, archiving, and backup procedures.

Think of data management as the care and maintenance of your treasures, ensuring they remain valuable and accessible.

Finally, don't forget about monitoring and optimization.

Think of monitoring as the compass that keeps you on course throughout your data journey.

Regularly assess the performance of your data acquisition strategy.

Are you achieving your objectives, or do you need to make adjustments?

Think of optimization as fine-tuning your approach to enhance efficiency and effectiveness.

Data acquisition planning is an ongoing process, not a one-time effort.

Think of it as an expedition where you continually refine your route, adapt to changing conditions, and discover new treasures along the way.

By following a well-structured data acquisition plan, you'll navigate the data landscape with purpose and clarity, uncover valuable insights, and achieve your objectives effectively.

Chapter 2: Reconnaissance and Initial Data Gathering

Let's embark on the initial reconnaissance steps, a pivotal phase in any information-gathering journey that lays the foundation for a successful mission. Think of these steps as the first few strides on a path that will lead you to valuable insights and data.

At this stage, you are setting the stage for your reconnaissance efforts, preparing to navigate the vast landscape of information that awaits.

Imagine these initial steps as the moment you put on your hiking boots, pack your essentials, and take that first step into the wilderness of data.

The first step in your reconnaissance journey is to define your objectives clearly.

Think of these objectives as the destination points on your map—where you intend to arrive after your journey.

What specific information or insights are you seeking? Are you looking for competitive intelligence, customer behavior patterns, or security vulnerabilities?

Imagine these objectives as the guiding stars that will lead you through the information landscape.

With your objectives in mind, it's time to identify the sources of information that will be most valuable to you.

Think of these sources as the rivers and streams you'll follow as you navigate the data landscape.

Consider both internal and external sources—internal databases, customer feedback, social media, public records, and more.

Imagine these sources as the diverse terrain you'll traverse in your quest for information.

Once you've identified your sources, it's essential to gather and organize the tools you'll need for your reconnaissance.

Think of these tools as the equipment you pack for your journey, each serving a specific purpose.

These tools may include data scraping software, analytics platforms, search engines, and specialized research databases.

Imagine these tools as the compasses, maps, and GPS devices that will help you navigate the data wilderness.

Now, let's delve into the importance of understanding your target audience or subject.

Think of this step as getting to know the locals and understanding their customs and language.

Whether you're collecting market data, researching competitors, or assessing security vulnerabilities, understanding the context is crucial.

Imagine it as learning the lay of the land and the behavior of the inhabitants.

Consider the demographics, preferences, and behaviors of your target audience.

Think of these factors as the cultural nuances and local customs that influence your interactions.

Understanding the context and the people involved will help you tailor your reconnaissance efforts and make your journey more productive.

As you embark on your reconnaissance mission, consider the types of information you aim to gather.

Think of these types as the landmarks and features you want to identify along the way.

Are you looking for quantitative data, such as sales figures, or qualitative insights, like customer testimonials?

Do you need real-time data, historical records, or projections for the future?

Imagine these types of information as the different terrains you'll traverse during your journey.

With your objectives, sources, tools, and target audience in mind, it's time to plan your reconnaissance strategy.

Think of this strategy as your route map, detailing the path you'll take to reach your destination.

Consider the sequence of actions you'll perform, the order in which you'll gather information, and the methods you'll use.

Imagine this strategy as the roadmap that will keep you on track and ensure a systematic approach.

Remember that reconnaissance is not a one-time effort but an ongoing process.

Think of it as an expedition where you continually gather information, adapt to changing conditions, and refine your strategy.

Regularly assess your progress, evaluate the effectiveness of your methods, and adjust your approach as needed.

Imagine this as checking your compass to ensure you're heading in the right direction.

In the world of reconnaissance, data collection is a core activity.

Think of data collection as gathering treasures along the way, each piece of information adding value to your journey.

Consider the methods you'll use for data collection.

Will you conduct surveys, analyze online behavior, or extract data from various sources?

Think of these methods as the tools and techniques you'll use to collect the treasures you seek.

As you collect data, pay attention to data quality.

Think of data quality as the condition of the treasures you uncover.

Ensure that the data you gather is accurate, reliable, and free from errors.

Imagine it as polishing and preserving the treasures you've found, making them even more valuable.

Data analysis is the process of turning raw data into meaningful insights.

Think of data analysis as refining and shaping the treasures you've collected, transforming them into valuable gems.

Consider the analytical techniques you'll use.

Will you perform statistical analysis, data visualization, or machine learning algorithms?

Think of these techniques as the tools that will help you unlock the hidden potential within your data.

Interpret the results of your analysis in the context of your objectives.

Think of interpretation as understanding the stories and meanings behind the gems you've discovered.

What do the patterns and trends in your data reveal? How do they align with your goals?

Imagine interpretation as deciphering the messages and narratives hidden within your data.

With your insights in hand, it's time to communicate your findings effectively.

Think of communication as the process of sharing your treasures with others, making them accessible and valuable to your team or organization.

Consider the best ways to present your insights.

Will you create reports, dashboards, presentations, or visualizations?

Think of these communication methods as the tools that will convey the beauty and significance of your gems to others.

Finally, remember that reconnaissance is an iterative process.

Think of it as an ongoing exploration, where you continually gather information, refine your strategies, and adapt to changing conditions.

Embrace the dynamic nature of data, and be prepared to make adjustments to your approach as new insights emerge.

Imagine reconnaissance as a journey filled with discoveries and insights, where each step brings you closer to achieving your objectives.

By following these initial reconnaissance steps with purpose and determination, you'll navigate the data landscape effectively, uncover valuable insights, and achieve your goals.

Let's dive into the fascinating world of passive and active data gathering techniques, essential skills for any information gatherer, whether you're an ethical hacker, a market researcher, or a competitive analyst.

Passive data gathering is like being a quiet observer, discreetly watching and listening without directly interacting with your target.

Imagine it as eavesdropping on a conversation, collecting valuable information without alerting anyone to your presence.

Passive techniques often involve monitoring publicly available data, such as website content, social media posts, or public records.

Think of it as silently collecting breadcrumbs of information left behind by your target.

By employing passive techniques, you can gather data discreetly and without raising any red flags.

Active data gathering, on the other hand, is more like engaging in a conversation with your target, directly interacting to obtain the information you need.

Imagine it as striking up a friendly chat, where you ask questions and engage in discussions to elicit valuable insights.

Active techniques can involve surveys, interviews, or direct data requests.

Think of it as actively seeking answers to your questions, engaging with your target to obtain the information you seek.

Each approach has its strengths and weaknesses, and the choice between passive and active techniques depends on your objectives and the context of your data gathering mission.

Passive techniques are excellent for collecting publicly available information without drawing attention to your activities.

Think of them as the stealthy approach, where you remain in the shadows while collecting valuable data.

Active techniques, on the other hand, allow you to interact directly with your target, providing opportunities to clarify information, ask specific questions, and gather data that may not be publicly accessible.

Think of them as the proactive approach, where you take the initiative to engage and elicit the information you need.

When choosing between passive and active techniques, consider the following factors:

Sensitivity of the data: Passive techniques are less intrusive and suitable for gathering publicly available information. Active techniques may be necessary for more sensitive or confidential data.

Access to the target: If you have access to the target and can engage in direct conversations, active techniques become more feasible. Passive techniques are useful when you have limited access.

Legal and ethical considerations: Ensure that your data gathering methods comply with relevant laws and ethical standards. Passive techniques are generally less likely to raise legal or ethical concerns.

Resource constraints: Passive techniques often require fewer resources, while active techniques may involve more effort, such as conducting interviews or surveys.

Let's explore some passive data gathering techniques in more detail.

One of the most common passive techniques is web scraping, where you automatically extract data from websites.

Imagine it as a digital spider crawling through the web, collecting information from web pages.

Web scraping can be used to gather data from various sources, such as news articles, product listings, or social media profiles.

Think of it as a way to efficiently collect publicly available data on a large scale.

Social media monitoring is another powerful passive technique.

Imagine it as keeping an eye on social gatherings, listening to what people are saying, and noting their interactions.

With social media monitoring, you can track mentions of your brand, monitor trends, and gain insights into public sentiment.

Think of it as a way to tap into the conversations happening in the digital world.

Public records research is a classic passive technique, akin to exploring an archive of documents and records.

Imagine it as sifting through historical records to find valuable information.

Public records can include court documents, property records, government reports, and more.

Think of it as uncovering hidden gems of information buried in the public domain.

Now, let's shift our focus to active data gathering techniques.

Surveys and questionnaires are versatile tools for collecting specific information directly from individuals or groups.

Imagine it as sending out a friendly questionnaire and receiving responses that provide valuable insights.

Surveys allow you to gather structured data, while open-ended questions in questionnaires can provide qualitative insights.

Think of them as interactive conversations with your target audience.

Interviews are like having in-depth discussions with experts, insiders, or individuals with relevant knowledge.

Imagine it as sitting down for a one-on-one conversation, where you ask probing questions and receive detailed answers.

Interviews can provide rich, context-rich information and allow for clarification of complex topics.

Think of them as opportunities to gain deeper insights through direct interactions.

Observational research involves actively observing and documenting behaviors, processes, or events.

Imagine it as being a participant-observer, immersing yourself in the environment to gather firsthand information.

Observational research can be particularly useful for studying real-world situations and behaviors.

Think of it as watching and learning from the actions and interactions of your subjects.

As you engage in data gathering, whether through passive or active techniques, keep in mind the importance of data quality.

Think of data quality as the clarity and accuracy of the information you collect.

Ensure that the data you gather is reliable, free from errors, and representative of your target population.

Think of it as ensuring that the puzzle pieces you collect fit together seamlessly to create a coherent picture.

In summary, mastering both passive and active data gathering techniques is essential for anyone seeking to uncover valuable insights and information.

Whether you're an ethical hacker conducting reconnaissance, a market researcher analyzing consumer behavior, or a competitive analyst tracking industry trends, the ability to gather data effectively is a valuable skill.

Think of it as equipping yourself with a versatile toolkit, allowing you to choose the right approach for each data gathering mission.

Remember that data gathering is not just about collecting information but also about understanding the context, assessing data quality, and communicating insights effectively.

Think of it as a holistic process that begins with clear objectives and ends with actionable insights that drive informed decisions.

By embracing both passive and active data gathering techniques, you'll be well-equipped to navigate the data landscape and unlock the secrets it holds.

Chapter 3: Advanced OSINT Techniques

Now that we've delved into passive and active data gathering techniques, it's time to explore the art of probing beyond surface-level information.

Imagine peeling back the layers of an onion to reveal the deeper, more meaningful insights hidden beneath.

Probing is about asking the right questions, seeking clarification, and digging deeper to uncover valuable data.

Think of it as the detective work of the information gathering world, where your curiosity and persistence lead the way.

Surface-level information is like the tip of an iceberg—visible, but only a fraction of what lies beneath.

Imagine you're in a vast ocean, and you want to explore what's beneath the surface.

Probing allows you to dive beneath the waves, exploring the depths to discover the hidden treasures of knowledge.

To probe effectively, you must be curious and inquisitive, eager to understand the context and motivations behind the data you encounter.

Think of yourself as an explorer, venturing into uncharted territory to make new discoveries.

Start by asking open-ended questions that invite detailed responses.

Imagine you're having a conversation with someone, and you want to encourage them to share their thoughts and experiences.

Open-ended questions begin with words like "how," "why," "what," and "tell me about."

These questions prompt your target to provide more than a simple "yes" or "no" answer.

Instead, they encourage them to share their insights, opinions, and personal experiences.

Consider these examples:

"How do you approach this particular problem?"

"Why do you think this trend is emerging in your industry?"

"What challenges have you encountered in your experience?"

"Tell me about a time when you faced a similar situation."

By asking open-ended questions, you create a space for rich, detailed responses that can provide valuable insights.

Think of it as giving your target room to share their expertise and perspective.

Active listening is a crucial skill when probing for deeper information.

Imagine you're not just hearing words but truly understanding the meaning behind them.

Active listening involves paying full attention to what your target is saying, empathizing with their perspective, and asking follow-up questions to gain a deeper understanding.

Think of it as being fully present in the moment, engaged in the conversation, and ready to explore further.

Body language, tone of voice, and non-verbal cues can also reveal valuable information.

Imagine you're not only listening to words but also observing gestures, expressions, and emotions.

These cues can provide additional context and insights into your target's thoughts and feelings.

Think of it as reading between the lines to uncover hidden meaning.

As you probe deeper, be prepared to adapt your questions based on the responses you receive.

Imagine you're following a winding path through a forest, and each turn reveals a new vista.

Your questions should evolve to explore the terrain as it unfolds.

Adapting your questions shows that you're engaged and genuinely interested in the conversation.

Think of it as a dynamic dance of inquiry, where your curiosity leads the way.

Avoid assumptions and confirmation bias.

Imagine you have a puzzle, and you're trying to fit pieces together.

Assumptions can lead you to force pieces into the wrong places, distorting the picture.

Confirmation bias is like only looking for pieces that match your preconceived image.

Instead, approach each data point with an open mind, willing to accept information that may challenge your initial assumptions.

Think of it as staying flexible and open to new perspectives.

Follow-up questions are your toolkit for deeper exploration.

Imagine you're on a treasure hunt, and each question is a clue that leads you closer to the prize.

Follow-up questions build on the information you've received, allowing you to explore specific details or nuances.

Think of it as peeling back the layers of an onion, revealing the complexities beneath.

Clarification questions are essential when dealing with complex or technical information.

Imagine you're translating a foreign language, and you want to ensure you understand the meaning correctly.

Clarification questions seek to eliminate any ambiguity or confusion.

Think of it as seeking clarity to prevent misunderstandings.

Summarize and reflect to confirm understanding.

Imagine you're looking in a mirror to ensure you have the right image.

Summarizing what you've heard and reflecting it back to your target confirms that you've grasped their message correctly.

Think of it as a feedback loop that ensures alignment in your understanding.

As you probe for deeper information, remember that patience is your ally.

Imagine you're on a quest, and each step takes you closer to your goal.

Patience allows you to explore thoroughly, giving your target the time they need to provide meaningful responses.

Think of it as allowing the story to unfold at its own pace.

Ultimately, probing beyond surface-level information is a skill that can unlock a world of valuable insights.

Imagine you're an explorer venturing into uncharted territory, equipped with a lantern to illuminate the hidden corners of knowledge.

Probing allows you to navigate the complexities of data gathering, revealing the depth and richness of the information you seek.

Think of it as an ongoing journey of discovery, where each question leads you closer to understanding and enlightenment.

By mastering the art of probing, you'll become a more effective information gatherer, capable of uncovering the hidden gems of knowledge that lie beneath the surface.

In the world of information gathering, exploiting Open Source Intelligence (OSINT) is a powerful strategy for collecting target data.

Think of OSINT as a vast treasure trove of publicly available information just waiting to be discovered.

Imagine you're setting out on a quest, armed with tools and techniques to extract valuable insights from the open, accessible sources on the internet.

OSINT encompasses a wide range of sources, from social media profiles to publicly available documents and everything in between.

Think of it as the digital breadcrumbs left behind by individuals, organizations, and entities.

To exploit OSINT effectively, you must first understand its scope and potential.

Imagine you're embarking on a journey, and a map of the OSINT landscape is your guide.

This map includes various categories of information sources, each offering unique opportunities for data collection.

Think of it as having a diverse toolbox at your disposal, with each tool designed for a specific purpose.

One of the primary categories of OSINT is social media intelligence.

Imagine you're peering into the lives and interactions of individuals and organizations through their social media profiles.

Social media platforms provide a wealth of information, from personal interests and connections to organizational affiliations and public statements.

Think of it as eavesdropping on conversations happening in the digital realm.

Social media intelligence allows you to gather insights into your target's activities, interests, and even their mindset.

Imagine you're sifting through a treasure chest filled with digital clues that can help you understand your target better.

By analyzing posts, comments, and interactions, you can piece together a more comprehensive profile of your target.

Think of it as assembling a mosaic of information, with each piece contributing to the larger picture.

Another crucial aspect of OSINT is online presence analysis.

Imagine you're conducting a thorough investigation into your target's digital footprint.

This includes websites, blogs, forums, and any other online platforms where your target may have a presence.

Think of it as exploring the digital landscape your target inhabits.

Online presence analysis allows you to uncover valuable data such as website content, blog posts, forum discussions, and more.

Imagine you're a detective, carefully examining the clues left behind in the digital realm.

These clues can reveal information about your target's interests, expertise, and even potential vulnerabilities.

Think of it as piecing together a puzzle to gain a deeper understanding.

OSINT also extends to publicly available documents and records.

Imagine you're delving into a treasure trove of government reports, academic papers, and public records.

These documents can provide valuable insights into your target's background, activities, and affiliations.

Think of it as accessing a library of information, with each document holding a piece of the puzzle.

Publicly available documents and records can offer a wealth of information, from financial disclosures to legal filings.

Imagine you're a researcher, uncovering critical data that can help you build a comprehensive profile of your target.

This type of OSINT can be particularly valuable when investigating organizations or individuals with a public presence.

Think of it as connecting the dots to reveal the bigger picture.

In addition to these categories, OSINT also includes domain and IP intelligence.

Imagine you're peering behind the curtain of websites and online infrastructure.

Domain and IP intelligence involves analyzing domain names, IP addresses, and hosting information to uncover hidden connections and vulnerabilities.

Think of it as exploring the infrastructure that supports your target's online presence.

This type of OSINT can reveal technical details, such as server locations and domain ownership, that may be crucial in your reconnaissance efforts.

OSINT is not just about collecting data; it's about transforming information into actionable intelligence.

Imagine you're a strategist, turning raw data into insights that drive your decision-making.

To exploit OSINT effectively, you must have the skills to analyze, interpret, and contextualize the information you gather.

Think of it as sharpening your analytical tools to extract the most value from your data.

OSINT also requires a strategic approach.

Imagine you're a chess player, carefully planning your moves to achieve your objectives.

A strategic mindset allows you to prioritize your data collection efforts, focusing on the most critical sources and information.

Think of it as a chessboard where each piece of OSINT is a potential move in your reconnaissance strategy.

Lastly, ethical considerations are paramount in OSINT.

Imagine you're an ethical hacker, committed to responsible and lawful information gathering.

Respecting privacy, following legal regulations, and adhering to ethical guidelines are fundamental principles in OSINT.

Think of it as navigating a moral compass that guides your actions and decisions.

Exploiting OSINT in target data collection is not just about acquiring information; it's about harnessing the power of publicly available data to gain a competitive edge.

Imagine you're an explorer, uncovering hidden treasures in the digital landscape.

With the right tools, techniques, and ethical approach, OSINT can be a valuable asset in your information gathering arsenal.

Think of it as a journey of discovery, where each piece of data brings you closer to your destination—a deeper understanding of your target and their world.

Chapter 4: Deep Web and Dark Web Investigations

Imagine venturing into a hidden realm, a part of the internet not indexed by traditional search engines.

The Deep Web, often shrouded in mystery, is a vast and enigmatic digital landscape.

Think of it as an underground network of websites and resources, not accessible through standard web searches.

Navigating the Deep Web requires a different set of skills and tools than the surface web, where most internet users spend their time.

Imagine you're embarking on an expedition, equipped with specialized gear to explore the uncharted territories of the digital world.

This journey involves understanding the Deep Web's structure and accessing its hidden corners.

Think of it as uncovering hidden treasures in a labyrinthine cave system.

The Deep Web is often misunderstood and associated with illegal activities, but it also serves legitimate purposes.

Imagine it as an iceberg, with the surface web representing the tip visible above the water, and the Deep Web, a massive portion concealed beneath.

One misconception is that the Deep Web is entirely nefarious, but in reality, it includes academic databases, private forums, and secure communication channels.

Think of it as a parallel universe of information and communication.

The first step in navigating the Deep Web is understanding its different layers.

Imagine it as an onion with multiple layers, each requiring specific techniques to access.

The first layer, known as the "surface Deep Web," includes legitimate websites that are not indexed by search engines for various reasons.

Think of it as a hidden garden within a larger, well-tended public park.

Accessing this layer may involve using search engines designed for Deep Web content or accessing websites directly.

Imagine you're uncovering hidden gems among the underbrush of the digital wilderness.

The next layer is the "deep Deep Web," which includes content protected by login credentials or restricted access.

Think of it as a gated community within the digital landscape.

Accessing this layer may require authentication, such as usernames and passwords, making it more challenging to explore.

Imagine you're attempting to enter a members-only club where access is carefully controlled.

Then there's the "dark web," the most mysterious and infamous part of the Deep Web.

Think of it as a shadowy underbelly, where anonymity is prized, and illicit activities can thrive.

Accessing the dark web involves using specialized software, such as Tor, which anonymizes your connection.

Imagine donning a mask and cloak to navigate the hidden alleys of a virtual city.

In the dark web, you'll find marketplaces for illegal goods, forums for cybercriminals, and anonymous communication channels.

Think of it as a digital marketplace for both legitimate and illicit transactions.

But it's essential to remember that not everything on the dark web is illegal or harmful.

Imagine it as a marketplace where you can find rare and exotic items, some of which are perfectly legal.

For example, whistleblowers and activists may use the dark web to communicate securely and protect their identities.

Think of it as a refuge for those who need to speak truth to power.

Navigating the Deep Web safely and responsibly requires specific precautions.

Imagine it as entering a foreign country where you need to respect local customs and laws.

Anonymity tools like Tor provide a layer of privacy, but they do not guarantee complete security.

Think of it as wearing a disguise in a foreign land; it conceals your identity, but you still need to be cautious.

Browsing the Deep Web should involve basic cybersecurity practices, such as using updated and secure software and avoiding suspicious links or downloads.

Imagine it as exploring a dense forest; you should watch out for potential dangers and tread carefully.

Remember that while the Deep Web can be a source of valuable information, it also hosts risks.

Think of it as an adventure filled with opportunities and challenges, where preparation and awareness are your best allies.

When it comes to searching for information on the Deep Web, specialized search engines like DuckDuckGo and NotEvil can be your guides.

Imagine them as the compass and map that help you navigate this uncharted territory.

These search engines focus on indexing Deep Web content, providing a gateway to the hidden information you seek.

Think of it as consulting an experienced guide who knows the ins and outs of the terrain.

Exploring the Deep Web can lead to discoveries beyond your imagination.

Imagine finding rare documents, obscure research, and communities of like-minded individuals.

Think of it as a treasure hunt where you unearth hidden gems that can enrich your knowledge and perspectives.

However, it's crucial to approach this journey with a sense of responsibility and ethics.

Imagine it as an expedition to a fragile ecosystem; your actions can have a significant impact.

Respect privacy and confidentiality, and avoid engaging in illegal activities or supporting malicious actors.

Think of it as being a responsible traveler who leaves only footprints and takes only memories.

In summary, navigating the Deep Web is like embarking on an exciting adventure into uncharted digital territories.

Imagine it as exploring a hidden world filled with both wonders and dangers.

With the right tools, knowledge, and ethical approach, you can unlock the secrets of the Deep Web and expand your horizons in the digital realm.

Think of it as setting sail on a voyage of discovery, where the journey itself is as rewarding as the destination.

Imagine a hidden marketplace, a virtual realm where transactions occur beyond the reach of traditional authorities.

The Dark Web, often associated with secrecy and illicit activities, is home to a multitude of marketplaces that operate in the shadows.

Think of it as a clandestine bazaar, where anonymity is the currency of trade.

These marketplaces exist within the encrypted and anonymous layers of the Dark Web, where users' identities are shielded.

Imagine it as a digital mask that conceals the faces of buyers and sellers alike.

While the Dark Web is often portrayed negatively due to its association with illegal goods and services, it's essential to recognize that it also serves legitimate purposes.

Think of it as a dual-edged sword, with both a dark side and a lawful one.

One common misconception is that the Dark Web is entirely nefarious, but in reality, it hosts a spectrum of activities.

Imagine it as a hidden city where some residents are law-abiding citizens, while others operate outside the law.

Some individuals use the Dark Web for privacy and security reasons, as it offers a level of anonymity difficult to achieve on the surface web.

Think of it as a haven for those seeking refuge from the prying eyes of surveillance.

Accessing the Dark Web typically involves using specialized software like Tor (The Onion Router), which routes internet traffic through a network of volunteer-operated servers.

Imagine it as a secret passageway that leads you into the heart of the Dark Web.

Once inside, you'll find a range of marketplaces catering to various needs.

Think of it as entering a bustling marketplace, but with hushed conversations and obscured faces.

Some of these marketplaces specialize in the sale of illegal drugs, weapons, counterfeit documents, and stolen data.

Imagine it as a black market where shadowy figures engage in covert transactions.

However, it's crucial to understand that not everything on the Dark Web is illegal or harmful.

Think of it as a marketplace where you can find rare and exotic items, some of which are perfectly legal.

For example, whistleblowers and activists may use the Dark Web to communicate securely and protect their identities.

Imagine it as a sanctuary for those who need to speak out against injustice.

Navigating the Dark Web requires a certain level of caution and awareness.

Think of it as venturing into a foreign land where danger may lurk in unexpected places.

While Tor provides anonymity, it does not guarantee complete security, and users must exercise caution.

Imagine it as wearing a disguise in a city where you're unfamiliar with the customs and laws.

When exploring Dark Web marketplaces, it's essential to remember the ethical and legal implications of your actions.

Think of it as abiding by a code of conduct, even in a world where rules are less clear.

Engaging in illegal activities on the Dark Web can have severe consequences, as law enforcement agencies monitor these spaces.

Imagine it as participating in an underground society with its own set of rules and consequences.

Despite the risks, there are legitimate reasons for visiting the Dark Web marketplaces.

Think of it as entering a hidden library with valuable information that cannot be found elsewhere.

For instance, researchers and journalists may use these marketplaces to access information and sources not available on the surface web.

Imagine it as a resource for those seeking to uncover hidden truths and stories.

One of the critical aspects of navigating the Dark Web is maintaining anonymity.

Think of it as a cloak of invisibility that shields you from prying eyes.

Users must be cautious about revealing personal information or engaging in conversations that could compromise their identity.

Imagine it as protecting your true identity while mingling with strangers in a crowd.

When accessing Dark Web marketplaces, users often encounter various cryptocurrencies like Bitcoin, which provide a degree of anonymity in financial transactions.

Think of it as using untraceable currency in a hidden economy.

This anonymity is essential for both buyers and sellers, as it shields their identities and helps maintain the secrecy of transactions.

Imagine it as using an unmarked envelope to send and receive payments.

However, it's crucial to recognize that the Dark Web's anonymity also attracts cybercriminals and malicious actors.

Think of it as a double-edged sword that can be wielded for good or ill.

In addition to marketplaces, the Dark Web hosts forums and communities dedicated to various topics.

Imagine it as a secret gathering of individuals with shared interests and concerns.

These communities may discuss technology, privacy, security, and even political activism.

Think of it as joining a group of like-minded individuals who value their online privacy.

As with any online space, the Dark Web has its own set of risks and challenges.

Imagine it as a digital wilderness, where you must be wary of potential dangers.

Malware, scams, and fraudulent schemes are prevalent, making it essential to exercise caution.

Think of it as navigating a treacherous path where hidden pitfalls await the unwary.

In summary, the Dark Web is a complex and multifaceted realm within the broader internet landscape.

Imagine it as a hidden world with both shadows and light.

While it is associated with illegal activities, it also serves legitimate purposes, offering privacy and anonymity to those who need it.

Think of it as a digital refuge for those seeking to protect their identities and communicate securely.

Navigating the Dark Web requires caution, ethical awareness, and a clear understanding of the potential risks and benefits.

Imagine it as embarking on a journey into the unknown, where your actions can shape your experience in this enigmatic digital realm.

In the end, it is up to individuals to decide how they will navigate and interact with the hidden corners of the Dark Web.

Chapter 5: Social Engineering and Targeted Attacks

Understanding the human mind is a pivotal aspect of social engineering.

Imagine it as delving into the intricacies of the human psyche to influence and manipulate.

Social engineers leverage psychological techniques to exploit human behavior, emotions, and cognitive biases.

Think of it as the art of persuasion, where words and actions are carefully crafted to achieve a desired outcome.

One fundamental concept in psychological manipulation is the concept of trust.

Imagine it as the foundation upon which all social engineering endeavors are built.

Establishing trust with the target is the first step in gaining their cooperation.

Think of it as the initial thread that weaves the fabric of deception.

Trust is often established through the use of pretexting, where the social engineer creates a plausible scenario or persona.

Imagine it as assuming a role or identity that the target finds believable.

Pretexting relies on the target's willingness to believe the fabricated story or persona.

Think of it as a well-acted performance that convinces the audience.

Another crucial psychological aspect is reciprocity.

Imagine it as the social contract that dictates that when someone does something for you, you feel compelled to reciprocate.

Social engineers exploit this innate human tendency by offering small favors or assistance.

Think of it as planting a seed of obligation in the target's mind.

Once the target feels indebted, they may be more willing to divulge information or cooperate.

Think of it as a subtle form of manipulation that relies on the target's sense of reciprocity.

Another psychological tool in the social engineer's arsenal is authority.

Imagine it as the influence that comes with perceived expertise or power.

By posing as an authority figure, social engineers can gain the trust and compliance of their targets.

Think of it as donning a uniform of credibility.

For example, a social engineer might impersonate an IT technician or a manager to gain access to sensitive information.

Think of it as exploiting the trust that individuals naturally place in authority figures.

Social engineers also rely on the principle of scarcity.

Imagine it as the desire for something that is perceived as rare or limited.

By creating a sense of urgency or scarcity, social engineers can manipulate their targets into taking action.

Think of it as dangling a coveted prize just out of reach.

For instance, a social engineer might claim that there's a limited-time offer or a unique opportunity.

Think of it as playing on the target's fear of missing out.

Reciprocity, authority, and scarcity are just a few of the psychological tactics employed by social engineers.

Imagine it as a toolbox filled with techniques designed to exploit human vulnerabilities.

Another essential concept in social engineering is persuasion.

Think of it as the art of convincing others to adopt a particular viewpoint or take a specific action.

Persuasion often relies on the principles of influence and manipulation.

Think of it as the strategic use of words and actions to guide someone's decisions.

One influential model of persuasion is the "Elaboration Likelihood Model" (ELM).

Imagine it as a framework that explains how people process and respond to persuasive messages.

ELM suggests two routes of persuasion: the central route and the peripheral route.

Think of it as two pathways to changing someone's attitude or behavior.

The central route involves careful and thoughtful consideration of the message's content.

Think of it as a deep dive into the facts and arguments presented.

In this route, people are motivated and capable of critically evaluating the information.

Think of it as the path taken when someone is engaged and attentive.

The peripheral route, on the other hand, relies on cues and shortcuts.

Imagine it as a surface-level evaluation that doesn't involve deep thinking.

In this route, people are influenced by peripheral factors such as the speaker's attractiveness or the emotional appeal of the message.

Think of it as the path taken when someone is not inclined to invest mental effort.

Social engineers often tailor their persuasion tactics to the route that is most likely to succeed with their target.

Imagine it as choosing the right approach to sway someone's opinion or behavior.

For example, if the target is highly motivated and knowledgeable, the central route might be more effective.

Think of it as presenting a well-reasoned argument backed by evidence.

However, if the target is not inclined to engage in critical thinking, the peripheral route may be the better option.

Think of it as using emotional appeals or superficial cues to influence.

Another critical aspect of persuasion is the concept of cognitive biases.

Imagine it as the shortcuts our brains use to process information and make decisions.

Cognitive biases can lead people to make irrational judgments and choices.

Think of it as the quirks and flaws in our mental processing.

Social engineers exploit these biases to manipulate their targets.

Think of it as leveraging the predictably irrational nature of human cognition.

One common cognitive bias is confirmation bias.

Imagine it as the tendency to seek out information that confirms our existing beliefs.

Social engineers can use this bias by providing information that aligns with the target's preconceived notions.

Think of it as reinforcing what the target already believes to be true.

Another prevalent bias is the authority bias.

Imagine it as the inclination to defer to experts or authority figures.

Social engineers can pose as authorities to gain the trust and compliance of their targets.

Think of it as taking advantage of the target's natural inclination to trust those in positions of power.

Other cognitive biases, such as the availability bias and the anchoring bias, also play a role in social engineering.

Imagine them as the mental shortcuts that can lead people to make predictable errors in judgment.

Social engineers are skilled at recognizing and exploiting these biases to achieve their goals.

Think of it as manipulating the quirks and idiosyncrasies of human thought.

In summary, social engineering is a sophisticated practice that relies on a deep understanding of psychology and persuasion.

Imagine it as a blend of psychology, persuasion, and manipulation.

Social engineers use a range of tactics, from building trust to leveraging cognitive biases, to achieve their objectives.

Think of it as a strategic game of influencing human behavior and decisions.

Understanding these psychological principles is crucial for both defending against social engineering attacks and recognizing when you might be the target of manipulation.

Think of it as equipping yourself with the knowledge to navigate the complex world of human interaction and influence.

Crafting targeted attack vectors is a nuanced skill that requires a deep understanding of the target, their vulnerabilities, and the methods of exploitation.

Imagine it as the art of creating the perfect strategy to breach a specific target.

A targeted attack vector is essentially the path or avenue through which an attacker gains access to a system or network.

Think of it as the entry point carefully designed to align with the target's weaknesses.

The first step in crafting a targeted attack vector is reconnaissance.

Imagine it as the detective work that precedes a heist.

In this phase, the attacker collects as much information as possible about the target.

Think of it as assembling the puzzle pieces needed to plan the perfect crime.

Reconnaissance involves passive and active information gathering, which we've discussed in earlier chapters.

Think of it as building a comprehensive profile of the target.

This includes identifying the target's vulnerabilities, potential entry points, and even the human factors at play.

Think of it as understanding the layout of the battlefield before launching an attack.

Once the reconnaissance phase is complete, the attacker can start crafting the attack vector.

Imagine it as a skilled architect designing the blueprint for a masterpiece.

The attack vector should be tailored to exploit the specific weaknesses identified during reconnaissance.

Think of it as selecting the perfect tool for the job.

For example, if the target is known to have unpatched software, the attack vector may involve exploiting known vulnerabilities in that software.

Think of it as choosing the lock that's most likely to open the door.

Social engineering can also play a significant role in crafting attack vectors.

Imagine it as the art of manipulating individuals to gain access to their secrets.

For instance, the attacker may impersonate a trusted colleague or send a convincing phishing email to trick the target into revealing sensitive information.

Think of it as using psychological tactics to bypass security measures.

The attack vector must align with the attacker's goals.

Imagine it as the plan that ensures all actions lead to the desired outcome.

For example, if the goal is to steal sensitive financial data, the attack vector may involve compromising a specific user account with access to that data.

Think of it as the path that leads to the treasure.

Once the attack vector is crafted, the attacker must test it to ensure its effectiveness.

Imagine it as a dress rehearsal before the big performance.

This testing phase, known as validation, involves simulating the attack to see if it successfully bypasses the target's defenses.

Think of it as fine-tuning the strategy before execution.

Validation is crucial because it helps identify any flaws or weaknesses in the attack vector.

Imagine it as ironing out wrinkles in a well-tailored suit.

If the validation reveals issues, the attacker may need to go back to the drawing board and refine the attack vector.

Think of it as making adjustments to the plan to ensure it works flawlessly.

Once the attack vector is validated, it's time for execution.

Imagine it as the moment when the curtains rise on a carefully rehearsed play.

The attacker deploys the attack vector with precision and stealth.

Think of it as executing a surgical strike on the target.

During execution, the attacker must remain adaptable and responsive to unforeseen circumstances.

Imagine it as a high-stakes game of chess where every move matters.

For example, if the target's defenses are stronger than anticipated, the attacker may need to pivot and explore alternative avenues.

Think of it as being prepared to switch tactics when the situation calls for it.

The attacker must also maintain operational security to avoid detection.

Imagine it as the criminal mastermind staying one step ahead of the authorities.

This includes covering tracks, using anonymizing tools, and minimizing any digital breadcrumbs.

Think of it as leaving no trace of the intrusion.

Once the attack is successful, the attacker can achieve their goals, whether it's stealing data, gaining unauthorized access, or causing disruption.

Imagine it as the moment when the treasure is finally within reach.

After the successful execution of the attack, the attacker may need to maintain persistence within the target's environment.

Think of it as securing a foothold to ensure continued access.

This may involve creating backdoors, establishing remote access points, or maintaining control over compromised accounts.

Think of it as ensuring the treasure remains in the attacker's hands.

Crafting targeted attack vectors is not a straightforward process.

Imagine it as a complex puzzle that requires careful planning, research, and adaptability.

It's a constant cat-and-mouse game where attackers seek to exploit vulnerabilities while defenders work tirelessly to secure their systems.

Think of it as a battle of wits in the ever-evolving landscape of cybersecurity.

In summary, crafting targeted attack vectors is a multifaceted endeavor that requires a deep understanding of the target, meticulous planning, and the ability to adapt to changing circumstances.

Think of it as the art of cyber warfare, where every move is strategic, and success depends on staying one step ahead.

Chapter 6: Network Mapping and Enumeration

Comprehensive network mapping techniques are essential in today's interconnected digital landscape.
Imagine it as creating a detailed map of a vast and intricate terrain.
These techniques involve the systematic exploration and documentation of a network's structure, devices, and connections.
Think of it as unraveling the intricate web of digital infrastructure.
Network mapping serves multiple purposes, including network optimization, security assessment, and troubleshooting.
Imagine it as a diagnostic tool for understanding the health of a network.
A comprehensive network map provides an overview of all devices within a network.
Think of it as a bird's-eye view of a bustling city.
It includes information such as IP addresses, hostnames, MAC addresses, and device types.
Imagine it as identifying the inhabitants and landmarks within the city.
One fundamental network mapping technique is network discovery.
Think of it as the process of uncovering hidden treasures within the network.
Network discovery involves identifying all devices connected to the network, whether they are computers, servers, routers, or IoT devices.
Imagine it as meeting and cataloging all the residents of the city.

This process is typically carried out using specialized software tools that send requests to devices, such as ICMP pings, to determine their presence.

Think of it as sending out invitations to a gathering.

Once the devices are discovered, the next step is to map their relationships and connections.

Imagine it as creating a social network graph of who knows whom.

This involves determining how devices are interconnected and which devices communicate with each other.

Think of it as understanding the relationships between individuals in the city.

Mapping network connections is crucial for understanding traffic flows and potential points of failure.

Imagine it as plotting the major roads and bridges in the city.

To perform comprehensive network mapping, various methods and tools are available.

Think of it as having a diverse set of tools in your toolkit.

One common method is active scanning, where network scanning tools, like Nmap, send probes to devices to collect information about their services and open ports.

Imagine it as a surveyor measuring the dimensions of buildings in the city.

Active scanning is useful for identifying active devices and open ports, which can be critical for security assessments.

Think of it as finding unlocked doors in the city.

Another method is passive network monitoring, which involves capturing and analyzing network traffic to build a map of device interactions.

Imagine it as eavesdropping on conversations in the city.

Passive monitoring can provide insights into the actual data flows within the network.

Think of it as listening to the city's conversations to understand its dynamics.

Comprehensive network mapping also extends to identifying vulnerabilities and potential security risks.

Imagine it as inspecting buildings for structural weaknesses.

Vulnerability scanning tools can be used to assess the security posture of devices and services within the network.

Think of it as checking for unlocked doors and weak locks in the city.

By combining network mapping with vulnerability assessment, organizations can prioritize and address security weaknesses effectively.

Imagine it as fixing the vulnerabilities to make the city safer.

Network mapping is not a one-time activity but an ongoing process.

Think of it as regularly updating the city map as new buildings and roads are constructed.

Networks evolve as new devices are added, configurations change, and security threats emerge.

Imagine it as the city growing and adapting to modern times.

Regularly updating the network map helps organizations maintain a current and accurate view of their digital landscape.

Think of it as keeping the city map up to date to reflect the changing urban environment.

In summary, comprehensive network mapping techniques are indispensable for understanding the structure, connections, and security of a network.

Think of it as the master key to unlocking insights into the digital world that organizations rely on.

These techniques enable organizations to optimize their networks, identify vulnerabilities, and ensure the smooth operation of their digital infrastructure.

Imagine it as the foundation for building a secure and efficient city of digital communication.

Enumerating assets and services is a crucial step in the reconnaissance process, where we dive deeper into understanding the digital landscape.

It's like exploring a treasure trove to discover what's hidden inside.

Asset enumeration involves identifying all the devices, systems, and resources within a network.

Think of it as creating a comprehensive inventory of what's in your digital toolkit.

This process goes beyond simply discovering devices; it's about categorizing them and understanding their roles.

Imagine it as not only finding tools in your toolkit but also knowing their purpose and functionality.

Assets can range from servers and workstations to routers, switches, printers, and IoT devices.

Think of it as identifying the various tools you have at your disposal.

By knowing what assets are present, you can better manage and secure them.

Imagine it as knowing where each tool belongs in your toolbox.

Service enumeration, on the other hand, focuses on identifying the services running on those assets.

Think of it as understanding the capabilities of each tool.

Services can include web servers, FTP servers, email servers, and various application-specific services.

Imagine it as knowing not just the type of tool but also its specific features.

Service enumeration provides insights into the software and protocols in use, which can be valuable for security assessments.

Think of it as understanding how each tool operates and communicates.

So, how do we go about enumerating assets and services effectively?

Think of it as embarking on a quest to uncover hidden treasures.

One common technique is to use network scanning tools like Nmap.

These tools send probes to devices to discover open ports and services.

Imagine it as sending out scouts to explore different parts of the treasure trove.

By analyzing the responses received, you can determine which services are running on each asset.

Think of it as the scouts reporting back with information about what they found.

Another approach is banner grabbing, where you interact with services to extract information about their versions and configurations.

Imagine it as striking up a conversation with the tool to learn more about it.

Banner grabbing can reveal valuable details, such as the web server type and version.

Think of it as asking the tool about its unique characteristics.

Enumerating assets and services is not limited to internal networks.

Think of it as exploring different territories to see what resources they offer.

External enumeration involves probing external-facing assets and services, such as websites and publicly accessible servers.

Imagine it as surveying the landscape beyond your immediate surroundings.

This is important for assessing the security of assets that are exposed to the internet.

Think of it as checking the security of your front gate.

Asset and service enumeration play a crucial role in vulnerability assessment.

Think of it as inspecting your tools to make sure they are in good working condition.

Once you know what assets and services are present, you can identify potential vulnerabilities and security risks.

Imagine it as checking your tools for wear and tear.

For example, if you discover an outdated web server version during service enumeration, you know that it may be susceptible to known vulnerabilities.

Think of it as recognizing that a tool needs maintenance.

In addition to identifying vulnerabilities, enumerating assets and services helps in network documentation.

Think of it as keeping a detailed catalog of your tools.

This documentation is invaluable for network administrators and security professionals.

Imagine it as having a user manual for each tool.

It provides a clear picture of the network's structure, which is essential for troubleshooting and network management.

Think of it as knowing where to find each tool when you need it.

Furthermore, asset and service enumeration can aid in access control.

Think of it as controlling who has access to your tools.

By knowing which assets and services are present, you can implement access control measures effectively.

Imagine it as locking certain tools away from unauthorized users.

For instance, you can restrict access to critical servers based on the information gathered during enumeration.

Think of it as allowing only trusted individuals to use the most important tools.

In summary, enumerating assets and services is a fundamental step in reconnaissance that allows us to uncover the treasures hidden within a network.

Think of it as the initial exploration of a vast and diverse landscape.

By understanding what assets and services are present, we can manage, secure, and optimize our digital resources effectively.

Imagine it as the key to unlocking the full potential of our digital toolkit and safeguarding it from potential threats.

Chapter 7: Exploiting Weaknesses: Vulnerability Assessment

Vulnerability scanning and analysis are essential components of the reconnaissance process, designed to uncover potential weaknesses within a system or network.

Think of it as running a thorough diagnostic checkup on your digital infrastructure.

In this chapter, we will explore the importance of vulnerability scanning, the techniques involved, and how to analyze the results effectively.

Imagine it as equipping yourself with the tools and knowledge to maintain the health of your digital environment.

Vulnerabilities, in the context of cybersecurity, are weaknesses or flaws in a system's design, implementation, or configuration that can be exploited by malicious actors.

Think of them as cracks in the armor of your digital fortress.

These vulnerabilities can exist in various elements of a network, including software, hardware, and even human processes.

Imagine it as identifying weak points in your security posture.

The consequences of leaving vulnerabilities unaddressed can be severe, as they can lead to security breaches, data leaks, and financial losses.

Think of it as neglecting to repair a leaky roof that could lead to damage inside your home.

To mitigate these risks, organizations and individuals must regularly assess their systems for vulnerabilities.

Imagine it as performing regular checkups to catch potential health issues early.

This is where vulnerability scanning comes into play.

Vulnerability scanning is the process of using automated tools and techniques to identify and assess vulnerabilities within a system or network.

Think of it as having a dedicated team of inspectors who examine every nook and cranny of your digital environment.

These tools actively probe the network, looking for known vulnerabilities, misconfigurations, and security weaknesses.

Imagine it as using specialized instruments to detect hidden problems.

There are various vulnerability scanning tools available, ranging from open-source options like OpenVAS and Nessus to commercial solutions.

Think of it as having a variety of diagnostic tools at your disposal, each with its own set of capabilities.

When conducting a vulnerability scan, the tool sends specific test packets or queries to the target system or network.

Think of it as a doctor using different diagnostic tests to check your health.

The responses received from the target are then analyzed to identify potential vulnerabilities.

Imagine it as the doctor interpreting test results to diagnose any health issues.

Vulnerability scanning can be categorized into two main types: unauthenticated and authenticated scanning.

Think of these as different levels of access during a medical examination.

Unauthenticated scanning is like examining a patient without access to their medical history.

This type of scanning assesses vulnerabilities from an external perspective, relying solely on publicly available information.

Think of it as identifying health problems without knowing the patient's medical history.

Authenticated scanning, on the other hand, is akin to a comprehensive medical examination with access to the patient's complete medical records.

This type of scanning requires valid credentials to access the target system or network.

Imagine it as having access to all relevant medical information for a thorough diagnosis.

Authenticated scans provide a more accurate assessment of vulnerabilities because they have a deeper understanding of the target's configuration and software.

Think of it as having access to a patient's complete medical history for a precise diagnosis.

Now, let's discuss the process of vulnerability scanning in more detail.

Think of it as breaking down the steps of a medical examination.

Preparation: Before conducting a vulnerability scan, it's essential to define the scope of the assessment.

Think of it as deciding which areas of the body to focus on during a medical checkup.

Determine the target systems or network segments to be scanned and obtain any necessary permissions.

Imagine it as getting consent from the patient for specific tests.

Scanning: The scanning tool is configured with the target's IP addresses and other relevant information.

Think of it as preparing the equipment for a medical test.

The tool then initiates the scan, sending test packets or queries to the target.

Imagine it as the doctor performing tests and examinations.

Detection: During the scanning process, the tool detects open ports, services, and potential vulnerabilities.

Think of it as identifying abnormalities or issues in the patient's test results.

It compares the collected data against a database of known vulnerabilities.

Imagine it as comparing test results to a medical database of symptoms and conditions.

Reporting: Once the scan is complete, the tool generates a report that details the vulnerabilities found, their severity, and recommended actions for mitigation.

Think of it as the doctor providing a diagnosis and treatment plan.

This report is crucial for organizations to prioritize and address vulnerabilities effectively.

Imagine it as receiving a medical report with recommendations for treatment.

Remediation: After vulnerabilities are identified, the next step is remediation, which involves taking action to fix or mitigate the issues.

Think of it as following the doctor's treatment plan to recover from an illness.

This can include applying patches, reconfiguring systems, or implementing security measures.

Imagine it as undergoing treatment and making lifestyle changes for better health.

Validation: After remediation, it's essential to validate that the vulnerabilities have been addressed.

Think of it as going for a follow-up medical checkup to ensure the treatment was successful.

This may involve re-scanning the system to confirm that the vulnerabilities are no longer present.

Imagine it as verifying that the health issue has been resolved.

Continuous Monitoring: Vulnerability scanning is not a one-time task but an ongoing process.

Think of it as adopting a healthy lifestyle to prevent future health problems.

Regular scans and continuous monitoring help organizations stay ahead of emerging threats and vulnerabilities.

Imagine it as maintaining good health practices to prevent illness.

In summary, vulnerability scanning and analysis are vital components of cybersecurity, akin to regular medical checkups for our digital environments.

By proactively identifying and addressing vulnerabilities, organizations and individuals can strengthen their security posture and protect against potential threats.

Think of it as adopting a preventive healthcare approach to ensure the long-term health and well-being of your digital assets.

Next, we'll delve into the crucial topic of exploiting discovered vulnerabilities, which is a pivotal phase in the ethical hacking and cybersecurity journey.

Imagine this phase as a critical mission in which you, as an ethical hacker or security professional, actively leverage the vulnerabilities you've uncovered during reconnaissance and vulnerability scanning.

Think of it as a skilled surgeon using their knowledge to perform a precise and controlled procedure.

Now, why is this phase so important? Well, while finding vulnerabilities is essential, understanding how to exploit them is equally critical.

Consider it akin to discovering a hidden entrance to a fortress; knowing it exists is not enough—you need to know how to access it.

Exploiting vulnerabilities allows ethical hackers to simulate real-world attack scenarios and understand the potential impact of these vulnerabilities on the security of a system or network.

Imagine it as a fire drill for your cybersecurity measures; you need to know how the system responds to different types of threats.

To execute successful vulnerability exploitation, you'll need a deep understanding of the vulnerabilities themselves, the systems they affect, and the tools and techniques required for exploitation.

Think of it as mastering the specific skills needed for each type of surgery.

But hold on, you might ask, "Why would ethical hackers want to exploit vulnerabilities?" Well, there are several valid reasons.

First, by actively exploiting vulnerabilities, ethical hackers can demonstrate the real risk posed by these weaknesses to system owners and stakeholders.

Imagine it as showing an x-ray to a patient to explain the severity of a medical condition.

This visual representation of the potential damage can be a powerful tool for convincing organizations to take security measures seriously.

Second, exploitation allows ethical hackers to test the effectiveness of existing security controls.

Consider it as pressure-testing a security system to see if it holds up under attack.

By attempting to exploit vulnerabilities, you can assess whether the security measures in place are robust enough to detect and respond to threats.

Additionally, ethical hackers can use exploitation as a means to gather further information about a system or network.

Think of it as a detective collecting evidence to solve a complex case.

By exploiting vulnerabilities, you may uncover hidden data, gain unauthorized access to systems, or even pivot to other parts of the network, providing valuable insights into the security landscape.

Now, let's discuss the steps and considerations involved in exploiting vulnerabilities effectively.

Think of these steps as the precise surgical procedure that must be followed.

Identify Target Systems: Begin by identifying the specific systems or components you intend to exploit. Not all vulnerabilities are relevant to your goals, so focus on those that align with your objectives.

Imagine it as selecting the right patient for surgery based on their condition.

Understand the Vulnerability: Before attempting exploitation, thoroughly understand the vulnerability you plan to target. Study its characteristics, potential impact, and any known exploits.

Think of it as reviewing a patient's medical history and the details of their condition.

Gather Exploitation Tools: Just as a surgeon prepares their surgical instruments, gather the necessary tools for exploitation. These may include exploit frameworks, scripts, or specialized software.

Imagine it as having a set of specialized tools for different surgical procedures.

Plan and Test: Develop a detailed plan for the exploitation attempt. Consider factors such as potential risks, consequences, and the need for backup measures. Test your plan in a controlled environment before conducting the actual exploitation.

Think of this as a surgeon rehearsing a complex surgery in a simulation.

Execute Exploitation: When ready, execute the exploitation attempt following your plan. Monitor the process closely and be prepared to adapt if unexpected challenges arise.

Imagine it as performing a precise surgical procedure with a team of skilled professionals.

Document the Process: Throughout the exploitation, document every step, including the tools used, commands executed, and the results obtained. This documentation is crucial for later analysis and reporting.

Think of this as maintaining detailed medical records during surgery.

Assess Impact: After successful exploitation or when the attempt reaches its conclusion, assess the impact on the target system or network. Understand what level of access or control you've gained.

Consider it as evaluating the patient's response to surgery and monitoring their recovery.

Report Findings: Just as a surgeon provides a detailed report to the patient and their family, create a comprehensive report of the exploitation attempt. Include all relevant details, vulnerabilities exploited, and potential risks.

Think of this as sharing the results of a medical procedure and discussing the patient's prognosis.

Recommend Remediation: Along with your findings, provide recommendations for remediation. Suggest steps to address the exploited vulnerabilities and enhance the overall security posture.

Imagine it as prescribing a treatment plan and lifestyle changes for a patient's recovery.

Maintain Ethics and Legal Compliance: Always ensure that your exploitation attempts are conducted within the bounds of ethical hacking and legal frameworks. Unauthorized or malicious exploitation can have serious consequences.

Think of this as adhering to medical ethics and legal regulations in the field of healthcare.

In summary, exploiting vulnerabilities is a critical phase in the ethical hacking process, enabling security professionals to assess risks, test security controls, and gather valuable insights.

Think of it as the intricate surgery required to restore and enhance the health of digital systems and networks.

By following ethical guidelines, documenting findings, and providing remediation recommendations, ethical hackers play a crucial role in strengthening cybersecurity defenses and protecting against real-world threats.

Chapter 8: Data Exfiltration Methods

In this chapter, we'll delve into the intriguing world of covert data exfiltration techniques. This is a topic that will take us into the realm of espionage and undercover operations in the digital landscape.

Imagine covert data exfiltration as the art of secretly and stealthily extracting sensitive information from a target system or network without alerting security measures or raising suspicion.

Think of it as the digital equivalent of a secret agent slipping unnoticed through the shadows.

Now, you might wonder, "Why do we need covert data exfiltration techniques?" Well, there are legitimate reasons for security professionals and ethical hackers to explore this area.

First and foremost, understanding covert data exfiltration is essential for testing the effectiveness of an organization's security measures. By simulating real-world scenarios where data is stealthily siphoned off, security experts can identify vulnerabilities and weaknesses that need to be addressed.

Consider it as staging a realistic burglary to test the security of a home.

Second, covert data exfiltration techniques can be used to demonstrate the potential risks to stakeholders and decision-makers within an organization.

Imagine it as a magician revealing the secrets behind a trick to educate the audience about the art of deception.

Third, these techniques can be valuable in penetration testing and red teaming exercises, where ethical hackers mimic malicious actors to evaluate an organization's readiness and response capabilities.

Think of it as a martial artist sparring with a partner to improve their combat skills.

With that understanding, let's explore some covert data exfiltration techniques:

Covert Channels: Covert channels are hidden pathways within a network or system that allow data to be transferred discreetly. These channels can exploit unused or obscure communication methods, making detection challenging.

Think of covert channels as secret tunnels in a fortress that only a select few know about.

Steganography: Steganography involves hiding data within other files or media, such as images or audio. By imperceptibly altering the least significant bits of a file, information can be concealed within it.

Imagine it as hiding a message within a painting by subtly changing the colors of individual pixels.

Low and Slow Techniques: Rather than sending large amounts of data quickly, low and slow techniques spread data exfiltration over an extended period, making it less conspicuous. This can involve sending small chunks of data at irregular intervals.

Think of it as a thief stealing a single coin at a time over weeks, avoiding suspicion.

DNS Tunneling: DNS (Domain Name System) tunneling utilizes DNS requests and responses to transmit data. Attackers can encode information within DNS queries, making it appear as regular traffic.

Imagine it as encoding messages in the addresses on envelopes to bypass postal security.

Traffic Manipulation: Manipulating regular network traffic to hide data exfiltration is another covert technique. For instance, altering the timing of data packets or embedding data within seemingly innocuous traffic can be used to exfiltrate data.

Think of it as embedding a secret message in a crowded conversation, making it difficult to discern.

Cloud-Based Exfiltration: Attackers may use cloud-based storage or services to exfiltrate data. By encrypting and uploading sensitive information to cloud platforms, they can access it from anywhere, making detection more challenging.

Imagine it as storing valuables in a secure vault away from the scene of a heist.

Protocol Manipulation: Manipulating application-layer protocols like HTTP or HTTPS can be used to hide data exfiltration. Attackers can encode information within legitimate-looking requests or responses.

Think of it as concealing a message within a conversation by using code words and subtle cues.

Compression and Encryption: Compressing and encrypting data before exfiltration can make it appear as random noise to security monitoring systems. Only those with the decryption key can reconstruct the original information.

Imagine it as writing a message in a secret code that only a trusted recipient can decipher.

Social Engineering: Social engineering techniques can be employed to trick individuals with access to sensitive data into unknowingly facilitating its exfiltration. This might involve phishing emails, pretexting, or other manipulative tactics.

Think of it as convincing a gatekeeper to grant access to a restricted area through charm and deception.

Data Fragmentation: Breaking data into small fragments and sending them through different channels or at different times can make detection challenging. Once all fragments are collected, the attacker can reconstruct the original information.

Imagine it as sending pieces of a puzzle separately and assembling them later to reveal the complete picture.

In summary, covert data exfiltration techniques are a vital aspect of ethical hacking and cybersecurity. Understanding these techniques is essential for identifying vulnerabilities, assessing security measures, and educating organizations about potential risks.

Think of it as the art of stealth and subterfuge in the world of digital security, where knowledge is the key to defending against covert threats.

Next, we'll explore the crucial topic of encrypting and hiding stolen data, which is an essential skill for both ethical hackers and cybercriminals. While we always advocate ethical practices, it's essential to understand these techniques to protect against them.

Imagine a scenario where an attacker successfully breaches a target's defenses and gains access to sensitive data. This data could be anything from financial records to personal information or classified documents. The question then becomes, how can this stolen data be secured and hidden from detection?

Encryption is a fundamental tool in this endeavor. It involves the transformation of data into a coded format that can only be decrypted with the appropriate encryption key. Without the key, even if the data is intercepted or accessed, it remains gibberish to anyone who tries to read it.

Think of encryption as a secret language known only to the sender and receiver, rendering the intercepted message meaningless to eavesdroppers.

There are two primary types of encryption: symmetric and asymmetric. In symmetric encryption, the same key is used for both encryption and decryption. This method is efficient but requires secure key distribution, which can be a challenge.

Imagine it as a lock that can be opened and closed with the same key, but you must ensure that only the intended recipient possesses that key.

On the other hand, asymmetric encryption, also known as public-key encryption, uses a pair of keys: a public key for encryption and a private key for decryption. This approach eliminates the need for secure key exchange, making it more practical for secure communication.

Think of it as a magical lock where anyone can put a message inside (using the public key), but only the person with the special key (the private key) can open it.

In the context of hiding stolen data, encryption can be employed to secure the information while it's in transit or at rest. Attackers may use strong encryption algorithms to make sure that even if their activities are detected, the stolen data remains inaccessible to anyone who intercepts it. But encryption alone may not be enough. Cybercriminals often employ additional techniques to hide their tracks and ensure that their activities go undetected. Let's delve into some of these tactics:

Steganography: We mentioned steganography earlier when discussing covert data exfiltration. It involves hiding data within other files or media, making it virtually invisible. For instance, an attacker might embed stolen data within the pixels of an innocuous image file.

Think of it as hiding a needle in a haystack, where the needle represents the stolen data, and the haystack is the cover file.

Data Fragmentation: Instead of sending or storing the stolen data as a whole, attackers may break it into smaller, more manageable fragments. These fragments can be distributed across multiple locations, making it difficult for security systems to detect and reconstruct the complete data.

Imagine it as scattering puzzle pieces across various rooms, with each piece too small to reveal the full picture.

File Obfuscation: Attackers can change file extensions or use deceptive file names to make stolen data appear as something innocuous. For example, they might rename a sensitive document to look like a benign system file.

Think of it as a spy disguising themselves as a janitor to move through a secure facility unnoticed.

Traffic Anonymization: When exfiltrating stolen data, cybercriminals may route their traffic through anonymization networks like Tor or VPNs. This masks the source of the traffic, making it challenging for investigators to trace it back to the attacker.

Imagine it as a getaway car with tinted windows, making it impossible to identify the driver.

Data Encryption with Hidden Keys: To further complicate matters, attackers may encrypt stolen data using strong encryption and then hide the encryption keys in different locations. Without these keys, even if investigators find the encrypted data, they won't be able to decrypt it.

Think of it as a treasure hunt where the map is divided into pieces, with each piece hidden separately.

Time Delayed Data Exfiltration: Attackers might intentionally delay the exfiltration of stolen data, spreading it out over an extended period. This delay reduces the chances of detection, as security systems may not flag small, sporadic data transfers.

Imagine it as a thief stealing one piece of jewelry per week to avoid suspicion.

Bursts of Activity: In contrast to time-delayed exfiltration, attackers may use bursts of activity to transfer stolen data quickly, overwhelming security systems and diverting attention.

Think of it as a magician creating a diversion by producing a flurry of doves while the real trick happens unnoticed.

By combining encryption with these tactics, cybercriminals can make it exceptionally challenging for organizations to detect and respond to data breaches. Ethical hackers and cybersecurity professionals must be aware of these techniques to counter them effectively.

In the ongoing digital cat-and-mouse game, staying informed and vigilant is the key to securing sensitive information and preventing it from falling into the wrong hands.

Chapter 9: Evading Detection and Covering Tracks

Next, we delve into the intriguing and sometimes shadowy world of anti-forensics techniques. While the term "forensics" may conjure images of crime scene investigations and solving mysteries, in the realm of cybersecurity, it takes on a different meaning. Cyber forensics involves the systematic collection, analysis, and preservation of digital evidence for investigative purposes. It's a crucial field in tracking down cybercriminals and understanding the scope of digital incidents.

However, just as there are those who investigate and analyze digital activities, there are also individuals who seek to evade detection and cover their tracks. These individuals employ anti-forensics techniques to thwart cyber forensic investigations and erase digital footprints.

Imagine a scenario where a cybercriminal has successfully infiltrated a network, stolen sensitive data, and left behind a trail of digital breadcrumbs. The cybersecurity team responsible for investigating the incident relies on digital forensics to uncover the who, what, and how of the attack. They painstakingly collect logs, examine system artifacts, and analyze network traffic to piece together the puzzle.

This is where anti-forensics comes into play. It's the art of subverting these investigative efforts and making it as challenging as possible to trace the steps of the attacker. While anti-forensics techniques have legitimate applications in the cybersecurity world, such as testing the resilience of security measures, they can also be used by malicious actors to cover their tracks.

One of the primary anti-forensics techniques is data destruction. Imagine a scenario where a cybercriminal realizes they've been detected. In a frantic bid to erase any evidence of their presence, they may employ various methods to destroy data on compromised systems. This could involve wiping hard drives, deleting log files, or even physically damaging hardware.

Think of it as someone setting fire to a trail of documents to destroy incriminating evidence. In the digital realm, data destruction can be just as effective at obscuring the truth.

Another common anti-forensics technique is the use of encryption. Cybercriminals may encrypt sensitive data or communication to ensure that, even if investigators gain access, they can't decipher the information. Encryption makes it appear as if the data is gibberish, rendering it useless without the decryption key.

Picture it as writing a secret message in code. Without the key, it's nearly impossible to decipher the hidden message.

Steganography is yet another technique employed by those seeking to evade forensic scrutiny. It involves hiding data within other files or media in such a way that it's virtually undetectable. For instance, an attacker might embed stolen data within the pixels of an innocuous image file.

Think of it as hiding a treasure chest beneath the floorboards, with no visible sign of its presence.

Anti-forensics can also involve altering timestamps and metadata associated with files and activities. By manipulating these details, cybercriminals can create confusion and mislead investigators about the timing and origin of digital artifacts.

Imagine it as someone tampering with the date and time on a security camera to provide a false alibi.

Covering one's tracks often extends to erasing or altering log files, which can provide a trail of system activity. Attackers may delete or modify these logs to remove any evidence of their actions.

Think of it as an intruder wiping their fingerprints from the scene of a crime.

To make matters more challenging for digital investigators, anti-forensics can also involve techniques like data obfuscation and fragmentation. These tactics make it difficult to reconstruct the full picture of an attack, as pieces of the puzzle are scattered, distorted, or hidden.

Imagine it as tearing a document into shreds and scattering them in different locations, making it nearly impossible to read.

Despite the effectiveness of these anti-forensics techniques, cybersecurity professionals continually evolve their forensic methodologies to counter them. The cat-and-mouse game between cybercriminals and defenders persists, pushing both sides to innovate.

Ethical hackers and digital investigators must stay updated on the latest anti-forensics tactics to develop robust countermeasures. Ultimately, the goal is not just to uncover the truth but to safeguard digital assets and protect against malicious actors who seek to exploit vulnerabilities in our increasingly interconnected world.

In the world of cybersecurity and reconnaissance, staying hidden and maintaining covert communication channels is of paramount importance. Imagine a scenario where ethical hackers or intelligence operatives need to exchange information, but they must do so without attracting attention or detection by adversaries. This is where the concept of implementing stealthy communication channels comes into play.

Stealthy communication channels are ingenious methods used to transmit data or messages while minimizing the risk of detection. These channels are designed to operate quietly in the background, mimicking legitimate network traffic or appearing as innocuous data. The goal is to fly under the radar, ensuring that neither external attackers nor vigilant network defenders can easily spot the communication.

One common stealthy communication technique is known as "covert channels." These channels make use of unused or less-monitored parts of the network to transmit data. For example, hackers might exploit the time gaps between legitimate network traffic to insert their own data packets, effectively hiding their communication within the normal flow of network activity.

Think of it as sending a secret message by hiding it between the lines of a public conversation, making it nearly imperceptible to eavesdroppers.

Another method to implement stealthy communication is through "low-and-slow" techniques. This approach involves sending data at a deliberately slow pace to avoid triggering network anomaly detection systems. Imagine a hacker transmitting data at a rate that blends seamlessly with regular, slow network traffic, such as email or file transfers.

Picture it as quietly dropping pebbles into a pond instead of throwing a rock—minimal ripples attract less attention.

Steganography, a technique we discussed earlier in the context of anti-forensics, also plays a crucial role in stealthy communication. In this case, data is concealed within innocent-looking files or media, such as images or audio. By embedding messages within these files, operatives can exchange information covertly.

Think of it as having a conversation in plain sight by encoding messages in the background noise of a crowded room.

Communication over seemingly unrelated protocols is another strategy. Hackers may use protocols typically unrelated to data transfer, such as DNS (Domain Name System) or ICMP (Internet Control Message Protocol), to carry their covert messages. By exploiting the structure of these protocols, they can encode and decode information without raising suspicion.

Imagine it as having a secret conversation using hand signals in the midst of a loud and chaotic crowd.

Modern cryptography also plays a significant role in stealthy communication. Advanced encryption techniques ensure that even if intercepted, the content of the message remains unintelligible to unauthorized individuals. Moreover, cryptographic methods can help establish secure communication channels that are resistant to tampering or eavesdropping.

Think of it as locking your message in a secure box, ensuring that only those with the right key can access its contents.

The concept of "exfiltration" is closely related to stealthy communication. Exfiltration involves quietly siphoning data out of a target network or system. Hackers employ covert channels to exfiltrate sensitive information, and this process often involves multiple layers of obfuscation to avoid detection.

Picture it as carefully siphoning liquid from a container, ensuring not a drop is spilled or noticed.

Countermeasures against stealthy communication channels are an essential part of network defense. Network administrators and cybersecurity professionals deploy intrusion detection systems (IDS) and intrusion prevention systems (IPS) to monitor network traffic for signs of covert communication. These systems analyze network packets, looking for anomalies that might indicate hidden communication.

Think of it as having a watchful guard who spots the subtlest movements in a crowded marketplace.

Signature-based detection is one approach used by these systems, where known patterns or signatures associated with stealthy communication are identified and flagged.

Another method involves anomaly detection, where deviations from the norm trigger alarms.

Imagine it as recognizing an imposter in a crowd based on their suspicious behavior.

Ultimately, the world of stealthy communication channels is a cat-and-mouse game between those who seek to transmit data covertly and those who defend against such activities. As technology evolves, so do the methods employed on both sides of this digital battlefield.

In the end, whether you're a cybersecurity professional defending a network or an ethical hacker testing its resilience, understanding the intricacies of stealthy communication is essential in today's interconnected world. The ability to communicate securely and covertly can make all the difference in maintaining the upper hand in the ever-evolving landscape of cyber warfare.

Chapter 10: Legal and Ethical Considerations in Data Acquisition

In the realm of ethical hacking, having a structured framework and adherence to guidelines is of utmost importance. Ethical hackers, often referred to as "white hat" hackers, play a crucial role in securing systems and networks by identifying vulnerabilities before malicious hackers can exploit them. To effectively carry out their tasks, ethical hackers rely on established frameworks and guidelines that provide a systematic approach to ethical hacking.

One widely recognized framework is the "Certified Ethical Hacker" (CEH) framework, which is curated and maintained by the EC-Council. This framework offers a comprehensive approach to ethical hacking, encompassing various phases and methodologies. The CEH framework typically includes the following key phases:

Reconnaissance: In this initial phase, ethical hackers gather information about the target system or network. This includes passive information gathering, such as identifying public information available online, and active information gathering, which involves probing the target for vulnerabilities.

Enumeration: This phase involves actively probing the target to identify open ports, services, and possible vulnerabilities. Ethical hackers use tools and techniques to enumerate the target's resources and configurations.

Vulnerability Analysis: Once potential vulnerabilities are identified, ethical hackers analyze them to determine their severity and potential impact. This step is critical for prioritizing which vulnerabilities should be addressed first.

Exploitation: In this phase, ethical hackers attempt to exploit the identified vulnerabilities to gain unauthorized access. This step helps validate the severity of vulnerabilities and assess the potential impact of a real attack.

Post-Exploitation: After successful exploitation, ethical hackers explore the compromised system to understand the extent of access and the data they can access. This phase also includes maintaining access for further analysis.

Reporting: Ethical hackers compile detailed reports of their findings, including the vulnerabilities discovered, their severity, and recommendations for remediation. Clear and concise reporting is essential for organizations to address security weaknesses effectively.

Mitigation: Based on the ethical hacker's recommendations, the organization takes action to remediate the identified vulnerabilities. This often involves patching, reconfiguring systems, and implementing security best practices.

Reconnaissance (Revisit): After mitigation, ethical hackers may revisit the system to verify that the vulnerabilities have been addressed and that the security measures are effective. This helps ensure that no lingering issues remain.

Another widely adopted framework is the "Penetration Testing Execution Standard" (PTES). PTES provides a standardized approach to penetration testing, which is a subset of ethical hacking focused on identifying vulnerabilities through active exploitation. PTES consists of several phases, including pre-engagement interactions, intelligence gathering, threat modeling, vulnerability analysis, exploitation, post-exploitation, reporting, and cleanup.

It's important to note that ethical hacking frameworks emphasize responsible and lawful practices. Ethical hackers must obtain proper authorization and adhere to legal and ethical guidelines throughout their engagements. Unauthorized hacking, even with good intentions, can have serious legal consequences.

Guidelines and codes of ethics also play a significant role in ethical hacking. Organizations such as the EC-Council and the International Council of E-Commerce Consultants (EC-Council) have established codes of ethics for ethical hackers. These guidelines promote integrity, professionalism, and the responsible use of hacking skills for the benefit of cybersecurity.

Ethical hackers are expected to:

Obtain proper authorization before conducting any testing or assessments.

Respect the privacy and confidentiality of sensitive information.

Report findings responsibly and confidentially to the organization.

Use hacking skills only for legitimate and lawful purposes.

Continuously update their knowledge and skills to stay current with emerging threats and vulnerabilities.

In addition to established frameworks and guidelines, ethical hackers often draw from a vast toolbox of specialized tools and techniques. These tools include network scanners, vulnerability scanners, password cracking utilities, and exploit frameworks. Ethical hackers leverage these tools to identify and address weaknesses in target systems and networks.

Furthermore, ethical hacking is a dynamic field that constantly evolves in response to emerging threats and technology advancements. As new attack vectors and vulnerabilities emerge, ethical hackers must adapt and refine their methodologies to stay ahead of potential adversaries.

In summary, ethical hacking frameworks and guidelines provide a structured approach to identifying and mitigating cybersecurity vulnerabilities. These frameworks help ethical hackers systematically assess the security posture of organizations, enabling them to take proactive measures to protect their systems and data. Adherence to ethical guidelines and responsible hacking practices is crucial in maintaining the trust and integrity of the ethical hacking community and ensuring a safer digital environment for all.

Exploring the legal implications of data acquisition and handling is vital in the context of cybersecurity and ethical hacking. In an age where data is often described as the "new oil," understanding the legal boundaries and responsibilities associated with acquiring and managing data is paramount.

To begin, it's crucial to recognize that data can take many forms, including personal information, financial records, intellectual property, and more. Each category of data may be subject to specific legal regulations and protections, and ethical hackers must navigate this complex landscape with care.

One of the key legal frameworks that governs data handling is data protection and privacy laws. These laws, such as the European Union's General Data Protection Regulation (GDPR) and the California Consumer Privacy Act (CCPA), are designed to safeguard the privacy and rights of individuals whose data is collected and processed. Ethical hackers must be aware of these laws when conducting assessments that involve personal data, as non-compliance can result in severe penalties.

The GDPR, for instance, places strict requirements on organizations that handle the personal data of EU citizens. It mandates transparency in data processing, requiring organizations to inform individuals about how their data will be used. It also grants individuals the right to access their data and request its deletion under certain circumstances. Ethical hackers who encounter personal data during assessments must handle it with care and ensure it is not mishandled or exposed.

Additionally, data breach notification laws exist in many jurisdictions. These laws require organizations to promptly notify affected individuals and relevant authorities in the event of a data breach. Ethical hackers often play a critical role in helping organizations identify and address vulnerabilities that could lead to data breaches. Understanding data breach notification requirements is essential for ethical hackers, as their findings may trigger these legal obligations.

Intellectual property (IP) laws are another crucial aspect of data handling. Intellectual property encompasses patents, copyrights, trademarks, and trade secrets. When conducting assessments, ethical hackers may encounter proprietary software, code, or sensitive information that falls under IP protection. Unauthorized access or disclosure of IP can lead to legal action, so ethical hackers must treat such information with utmost confidentiality.

Another area of concern is the Computer Fraud and Abuse Act (CFAA) in the United States, which criminalizes unauthorized access to computer systems. Ethical hackers must obtain explicit authorization before probing systems, as unauthorized access can potentially lead to criminal charges.

Furthermore, contracts and agreements play a significant role in governing data acquisition and handling. Organizations often engage ethical hackers through legally binding contracts that outline the scope of work, confidentiality requirements, and other terms. These contracts may also include indemnification clauses to protect the organization in case of legal disputes arising from the assessment.

When conducting assessments, ethical hackers should maintain comprehensive records of their activities. Detailed documentation can serve as evidence of authorized testing and adherence to legal requirements. This documentation can be invaluable in the event of a legal inquiry or dispute.

Ethical hackers should also be aware of international data transfer regulations, as data often flows across borders. The transfer of data from one country to another may be subject to specific agreements and mechanisms, such as the EU-US Privacy Shield. Understanding these regulations is essential when dealing with multinational organizations or assessing systems that involve cross-border data transfers.

Additionally, the role of legal counsel in ethical hacking engagements cannot be overstated. Organizations should consult with legal experts who specialize in cybersecurity and data privacy to ensure that assessments are conducted in compliance with relevant laws and regulations. Legal guidance can help organizations navigate the complex legal landscape and mitigate potential risks.

In summary, ethical hackers must be well-versed in the legal implications of data acquisition and handling. Data protection and privacy laws, data breach notification requirements, intellectual property laws, and computer crime statutes are just a few aspects of the legal framework that ethical hackers must navigate. Engaging with legal experts and maintaining strict adherence to authorization and confidentiality requirements are essential steps in ensuring that ethical hacking activities remain within the bounds of the law. Ultimately, ethical hackers play a crucial role in helping organizations identify and address vulnerabilities while ensuring that data and legal obligations are handled responsibly.

BOOK 4
RECONNAISSANCE PRO
THE ULTIMATE HANDBOOK FOR ELITE INFORMATION
GATHERERS

ROB BOTWRIGHT

Chapter 1: The Art and Science of Elite Reconnaissance

Reconnaissance, often referred to as "recce" in military terminology, is a fundamental and essential discipline within the realm of cybersecurity.

At its core, reconnaissance involves the systematic gathering of information about an adversary, their capabilities, intentions, and vulnerabilities.

In the context of cybersecurity, reconnaissance serves as the initial phase of an operation, where cyber professionals gather intelligence about potential targets or threats.

Think of it as the first step in a strategic chess game, where understanding your opponent's moves and strengths is key to planning your own.

Reconnaissance is not limited to any one domain; rather, it encompasses a wide range of activities and techniques, both digital and non-digital, aimed at collecting valuable data.

In the digital realm, cyber professionals engage in reconnaissance to map out network structures, identify vulnerabilities, and gain insights into an organization's digital footprint.

This process involves passive and active information gathering, often relying on open source intelligence (OSINT), a wealth of publicly available data.

OSINT forms a critical component of reconnaissance, as it provides a treasure trove of information, such as domain names, IP addresses, and employee names, that can be used to build a comprehensive picture of an organization.

Reconnaissance is not a one-size-fits-all endeavor; it varies depending on the objectives and the nature of the target.

For instance, in the field of ethical hacking, reconnaissance plays a pivotal role in identifying potential weaknesses in an organization's security posture.

Ethical hackers, also known as white hat hackers, are cybersecurity professionals who use their skills to find and fix vulnerabilities before malicious hackers can exploit them.

Their reconnaissance efforts are conducted within the bounds of legality and ethical guidelines.

In contrast, malicious hackers, often referred to as black hat hackers, engage in reconnaissance to identify and exploit vulnerabilities for personal gain or malicious purposes.

Their activities are illegal and pose a significant threat to individuals and organizations.

To conduct effective reconnaissance, cyber professionals employ a wide array of tools and techniques, from network scanning to social engineering.

Each tool and technique is chosen strategically based on the objectives of the operation.

For example, network scanning tools like Nmap are used to identify open ports, services, and operating systems running on target systems.

This information is invaluable for understanding potential attack vectors.

In the realm of social engineering, reconnaissance often involves gathering information about individuals within an organization.

This could include identifying key decision-makers, learning about their interests, or even finding out their personal habits.

Social engineering reconnaissance helps malicious hackers craft convincing and tailored attacks, such as spear phishing.

In the world of nation-state cyber operations, reconnaissance takes on a different dimension.

Nation-states engage in sophisticated and often highly classified reconnaissance activities to gather intelligence on foreign governments, military capabilities, and critical infrastructure.

These activities can include cyber espionage, where reconnaissance focuses on infiltrating and exfiltrating sensitive data without detection.

In the context of corporate security, reconnaissance is used to protect valuable assets and data.

Companies invest heavily in cybersecurity measures to defend against potential threats, but understanding the tactics and motivations of adversaries is equally important.

Through reconnaissance, organizations can anticipate and proactively defend against cyberattacks.

However, reconnaissance is not limited to digital means alone.

In physical security, reconnaissance involves assessing vulnerabilities in buildings, facilities, and infrastructure.

Security professionals may conduct physical reconnaissance to identify weaknesses in access control, surveillance, or perimeter defenses.

This multifaceted approach to reconnaissance ensures a holistic understanding of security risks.

Moreover, reconnaissance is an ongoing process, not a one-time event.

In the dynamic landscape of cybersecurity, adversaries constantly evolve their tactics, techniques, and procedures.

To stay ahead, organizations must continuously gather intelligence and adapt their defenses.

This means regularly updating threat intelligence feeds, monitoring network traffic for suspicious activity, and conducting vulnerability assessments.

Ethical hackers, for instance, often perform periodic penetration tests to evaluate an organization's security posture.

These tests simulate real-world attacks and are based on the latest reconnaissance findings.

In summary, reconnaissance is a vital discipline in the field of cybersecurity, encompassing a wide range of activities and techniques to gather intelligence.

It serves as the foundation for understanding potential threats, vulnerabilities, and attack vectors.

Whether conducted by ethical hackers, nation-states, or corporate security teams, reconnaissance is an ongoing and adaptive process that plays a critical role in safeguarding digital and physical assets.

In advanced attack scenarios, reconnaissance takes on a heightened significance, serving as the foundation upon which the entire operation is built.

It's the critical first step that allows threat actors to identify and exploit vulnerabilities effectively.

In these scenarios, threat actors are often highly skilled, well-funded, and motivated to achieve their objectives.

They meticulously plan their attacks, and reconnaissance is the linchpin that enables them to do so.

Advanced attackers leverage both digital and physical reconnaissance techniques to gather intelligence about their targets.

They meticulously comb through publicly available information, often using advanced OSINT techniques to piece together a comprehensive profile of their target.

This can include details about an organization's employees, partners, technologies, and even its physical infrastructure.

With this information in hand, they can tailor their attack vectors to be highly convincing and effective.

In some cases, attackers may employ advanced web application reconnaissance techniques, probing websites and applications for vulnerabilities that can be exploited.

They may use tools like web application scanners to identify potential weaknesses in the software.

Advanced attackers are also adept at leveraging social engineering tactics during reconnaissance.

They may use spear-phishing emails that are highly personalized, making them more likely to trick the recipient into clicking on a malicious link or opening a malicious attachment.

These emails are crafted based on information gathered during reconnaissance, such as the target's interests, job role, and relationships.

In physical reconnaissance, advanced attackers may conduct on-site visits to gather additional intelligence.

They may scope out a target's physical location, assess security measures, and identify potential points of entry or weaknesses in the physical infrastructure.

Physical reconnaissance can be a critical component of an advanced attack, especially when the target's physical presence is essential to achieving the attacker's goals.

For instance, in the case of corporate espionage, knowing the layout of a target's office can aid in stealing physical documents or planting listening devices.

Additionally, advanced attackers may use deceptive reconnaissance tactics to throw off defenders and hide their true intentions.

They might intentionally leave false trails or create misleading digital footprints to divert attention from their actual objectives.

By doing so, they increase the chances of their reconnaissance activities going undetected.

Furthermore, advanced attackers often exploit zero-day vulnerabilities, which are previously unknown security flaws in software or hardware.

To discover and exploit these vulnerabilities, they may engage in extensive vulnerability research during the reconnaissance phase.

This involves reverse engineering software, analyzing network protocols, and scrutinizing code for potential weaknesses.

Advanced attackers understand that the success of their operations hinges on their ability to remain hidden and undetected.

Therefore, they take measures to minimize their digital footprint during reconnaissance.

They may route their activities through multiple proxies or VPNs, making it challenging for defenders to trace their actions back to their true source.

Advanced attackers also prioritize operational security (OPSEC) to avoid leaving behind any traces that could lead back to them.

This includes taking precautions like using disposable email addresses, encrypting communications, and securely storing any stolen data.

In summary, reconnaissance is a cornerstone of advanced attack scenarios, providing threat actors with the intelligence needed to execute highly targeted and effective operations.

It encompasses a wide range of digital and physical techniques, from OSINT and web application reconnaissance to social engineering and deceptive tactics.

For defenders, understanding the role of reconnaissance is crucial for detecting and mitigating advanced threats before they can achieve their objectives.

Chapter 2: Advanced Open Source Intelligence (OSINT)

In the world of cyber reconnaissance, Open Source Intelligence (OSINT) is a treasure trove of information that goes well beyond the basics.

Once you've mastered the fundamental techniques, you can delve into the more advanced aspects of OSINT to uncover even deeper insights.

Advanced OSINT practitioners understand that the internet is a vast and interconnected web of information waiting to be explored.

They know how to navigate this complex landscape to extract valuable data that can be used for various purposes, including cybersecurity, threat analysis, and investigations.

One of the key principles of advanced OSINT is the concept of "deep web" and "dark web" research.

While the surface web is accessible through traditional search engines, the deep web consists of web pages that are not indexed by search engines.

Advanced OSINT practitioners have techniques to access and explore the deep web, where they can find valuable information hidden from plain sight.

The dark web, on the other hand, is a part of the deep web that is intentionally hidden and requires specialized tools like Tor to access.

In the dark web, one can find marketplaces, forums, and communities where illegal activities are discussed and conducted.

Advanced OSINT practitioners are skilled at navigating the dark web safely and anonymously to gather intelligence on cybercriminal activities.

Beyond traditional search engines, advanced OSINT involves leveraging specialized search engines and databases that are not widely known to the public.

These tools allow practitioners to access a wealth of information that may not be easily discoverable through mainstream search engines.

Additionally, advanced OSINT practitioners know how to use advanced search operators and filters to refine their queries and uncover specific details about their targets.

They understand that the right combination of search operators can yield highly targeted and relevant results.

Social media analysis is another area where advanced OSINT shines.

While basic OSINT may involve simply observing public social media profiles, advanced practitioners take it a step further.

They use sophisticated tools to scrape and analyze social media data, tracking trends, sentiment, and even predicting future events based on online discussions.

Advanced OSINT practitioners are skilled at tracking online personas and understanding how individuals may use multiple accounts or pseudonyms to hide their true identities.

They can uncover connections between seemingly unrelated online profiles, providing valuable insights into an individual's online activities and associations.

Furthermore, advanced OSINT involves geospatial intelligence (GEOINT) techniques.

Practitioners can extract geolocation data from images, social media posts, and other online sources to map out the physical locations associated with a target.

This capability is crucial for tracking the movements of individuals or identifying potential physical security risks.

Another advanced OSINT skill is the analysis of metadata, which contains hidden information within digital files.

Advanced practitioners know how to extract and interpret metadata to gain insights into the origin and history of files, including who created them and when.

They can identify potential security risks, such as the inadvertent disclosure of sensitive information through metadata.

Furthermore, advanced OSINT practitioners often work in teams or communities where they can collaborate and share their expertise.

They understand the value of collective intelligence and know how to tap into the knowledge and resources of others in the field.

By combining their skills and resources, they can tackle complex OSINT challenges more effectively.

In summary, advanced OSINT goes beyond the basics, encompassing techniques and tools that allow practitioners to access the deep web, navigate the dark web, use specialized search engines, analyze social media, uncover geospatial intelligence, and interpret metadata.

It requires a high level of expertise and a commitment to continuous learning in the ever-evolving field of open source intelligence.

In the world of Open Source Intelligence (OSINT), automation and data analysis tools play a pivotal role in streamlining the information gathering process and extracting meaningful insights.

These tools are essential for advanced OSINT practitioners looking to efficiently collect, process, and analyze vast amounts of data available on the internet.

Automation in OSINT involves the use of scripts, software, and algorithms to perform repetitive tasks and gather information at scale.

One of the primary benefits of automation is its ability to save time and resources, enabling OSINT professionals to focus on higher-level analysis and decision-making.

Advanced OSINT practitioners often rely on web scraping tools that can automatically extract data from websites, forums, and social media platforms.

These tools can scrape text, images, and other media, allowing analysts to compile and analyze information quickly.

Additionally, automation tools can monitor websites and online sources for changes, alerting OSINT practitioners to updates or new content that may be relevant to their investigations.

Data analysis tools are equally critical in the advanced OSINT toolkit. They help make sense of the data collected and turn it into actionable intelligence.

One common type of data analysis tool used in OSINT is natural language processing (NLP) software. NLP can parse and understand text data, making it easier to identify key information, trends, and sentiment within large volumes of text.

Social media analysis tools equipped with sentiment analysis capabilities are valuable for tracking public sentiment and opinions about specific topics, brands, or individuals.

Furthermore, advanced OSINT practitioners use data visualization tools to create interactive graphs, charts, and maps that help them visually represent complex data patterns.

These visualizations can make it easier to identify connections, trends, and anomalies within the collected information.

Another crucial aspect of OSINT automation is the use of application programming interfaces (APIs) to access data from various online platforms and sources.

APIs allow OSINT practitioners to retrieve data directly from platforms like social media networks, search engines, and public databases.

Advanced OSINT practitioners understand how to work with APIs effectively, using them to collect data that may not be accessible through traditional web scraping methods.

Furthermore, machine learning and artificial intelligence (AI) play a growing role in automating OSINT tasks.

Machine learning algorithms can be trained to recognize patterns and anomalies within data, helping OSINT practitioners identify potential threats or opportunities more efficiently.

These algorithms can also assist in data classification, sentiment analysis, and even predictive analytics.

As OSINT automation tools and data analysis techniques continue to evolve, it's crucial for practitioners to stay updated with the latest developments in the field.

They must adapt to new platforms, data sources, and technologies to remain effective in their information gathering efforts.

Additionally, while automation and data analysis tools offer numerous benefits, they also come with ethical considerations.

Advanced OSINT practitioners need to be aware of privacy issues and data protection regulations, ensuring that their automated processes comply with legal and ethical standards.

Moreover, they must exercise discretion and responsible use of automation to avoid inadvertently spreading misinformation or engaging in harmful activities.

In summary, automation and data analysis tools are indispensable for advanced OSINT practitioners seeking to efficiently collect, process, and analyze large volumes of online information.

These tools save time, enable in-depth analysis, and provide valuable insights that can inform decision-making and investigations.

However, practitioners must also remain vigilant about ethical considerations and privacy concerns while harnessing the power of automation in the field of OSINT.

Chapter 3: Covert Social Engineering Techniques

In the realm of cybersecurity and ethical hacking, understanding advanced psychological manipulation strategies is essential for both defenders and ethical hackers. These strategies delve into the intricate world of human psychology, aiming to exploit cognitive biases and emotional triggers to achieve specific goals. Advanced psychological manipulation techniques build upon the foundational principles of social engineering, but they take the art of manipulation to a higher level of sophistication. One key strategy is the use of reciprocity, a deeply ingrained social norm where people tend to feel obligated to repay a favor or kindness. Ethical hackers and security professionals can use this principle by offering help or assistance to individuals within their target organizations, creating a sense of indebtedness that may be leveraged later. Another advanced technique involves exploiting authority figures and hierarchies within an organization. By posing as someone in a position of power or trust, a social engineer can influence individuals to divulge sensitive information or take actions they wouldn't typically consider. This strategy is particularly effective when hackers impersonate IT personnel or high-ranking executives. Furthermore, advanced psychological manipulation includes the use of scarcity as a persuasive tool. By creating a perception of limited availability or urgency, a social engineer can induce individuals to act quickly without fully considering the consequences. This tactic can be seen in phishing emails that claim an account will be locked unless immediate action is taken, prompting recipients to click on malicious links. Reciprocity, authority, and scarcity are just a few of the advanced psychological manipulation strategies used by ethical hackers to exploit human psychology. Understanding the concept of commitment and consistency is another essential tactic. Once an individual publicly commits to a particular course of action or belief, they are more likely to maintain that commitment, even if it contradicts their original stance. Ethical hackers can use this principle to manipulate individuals into revealing sensitive information by initially asking innocuous questions and gradually progressing to more probing inquiries. Moreover, the technique of social proof, which relies on the idea that people tend to follow the crowd, can be exploited. By presenting false evidence or fabricated testimonials that suggest others have already taken the desired action, a social engineer can influence individuals to follow suit. This is commonly seen in online scams that display fake user reviews or testimonials to lend credibility to a fraudulent product or service. The concept of liking is another powerful tool in the arsenal of advanced psychological manipulation. People are more likely to comply with requests from individuals they find likable, so social engineers often attempt to establish rapport and build trust with their targets. This can involve mirroring the target's behavior, interests, or beliefs to create a sense of familiarity and affinity. Furthermore, advanced manipulation strategies encompass the use of authority biases, where individuals tend to defer to experts or authoritative figures. Social engineers may impersonate industry experts or authoritative sources to gain the trust of their targets and persuade them to take specific actions. This technique is commonly employed in phishing campaigns where hackers pose as IT support personnel or security experts. Understanding the psychology of trust is crucial in advanced manipulation. Individuals tend to trust those who appear sincere, honest, and genuine. Social engineers often employ emotional appeals to create a sense of trust and empathy, making it easier to manipulate targets into providing sensitive information or cooperating with their requests. These emotional appeals may involve fabricated stories or scenarios designed to evoke sympathy or concern. Furthermore, advanced psychological manipulation includes the use of fear and intimidation. Creating a sense of urgency or impending danger can prompt individuals to act hastily without questioning the legitimacy of a request. This technique is prevalent in phishing emails that threaten dire consequences unless immediate action is taken. In summary, advanced psychological manipulation strategies are a critical component of social engineering and ethical hacking. Understanding how these strategies exploit human psychology can help defenders and ethical hackers develop more robust countermeasures and protect against manipulation attempts. By recognizing the tactics employed by social engineers, individuals and organizations can enhance their cybersecurity awareness and better safeguard sensitive information. In the world of cybersecurity, social engineering remains a potent and widely employed tactic, particularly in targeted campaigns. These campaigns are carefully crafted, often with specific objectives and tailored approaches to manipulate individuals or organizations. Unlike broad, indiscriminate attacks, targeted campaigns focus on exploiting the vulnerabilities of selected targets, making them a significant threat. One of the primary reasons targeted campaigns are so effective is the personalized nature of the attacks. Rather than casting a wide net, cybercriminals take the time to research and gather information about their intended victims. This research allows them to craft highly convincing messages and scenarios that are difficult to detect. The success of a targeted campaign often hinges on the attacker's ability to make the victim feel uniquely singled out. These campaigns often start with reconnaissance, where attackers collect information about the target, such as names, job titles, interests, and relationships. This information is then used to create tailored messages that seem genuine and believable. The attacker may impersonate someone the victim knows or trust, such as a colleague, boss, or family member. By using personal details and references, the attacker increases the likelihood of their victim falling for the ruse. The messages in targeted campaigns are carefully designed to manipulate emotions, whether it's fear, curiosity, or urgency. For example, an attacker might send an email that appears to be from the victim's HR department, informing them of a company policy change. The urgency and relevance of the message make the victim more likely to click on a malicious link or download a malware-laden attachment. Phishing emails are a common weapon in targeted campaigns, but they have evolved to be much more sophisticated than generic spam. They often contain no obvious red flags, such as misspellings or strange email addresses. The attacker's goal is to create an email that blends seamlessly with the victim's usual correspondence. Another tactic employed in targeted campaigns is pretexting. This involves the creation of a fabricated scenario that convinces the victim to divulge sensitive information or perform a specific action. For example, an attacker might impersonate a vendor and request login credentials to "update their records." Pretexting often relies on the attacker's ability to manipulate the victim's emotions, such as trust, fear, or a desire to be helpful. Spear phishing is another technique in targeted campaigns, where the attacker personalizes the phishing attempt to an individual or a group within an organization. By addressing the victim by name and referencing specific details, such as recent projects or events, the attacker increases the chances of success. Social engineering in targeted campaigns can extend beyond emails. Attackers may also use phone calls, social media, or even physical visits to manipulate their victims. In some cases, the attacker may engage in a long-term effort to build rapport and trust with the victim before exploiting it. This can involve creating fake online personas or infiltrating social circles. For example, an attacker may pose as a new employee and spend months integrating themselves into the company culture before launching an attack. Targeted campaigns can have devastating consequences, as they often result in successful data breaches, financial losses, or reputational damage. Even well-trained individuals can fall victim to these attacks, highlighting the importance of robust cybersecurity awareness. Organizations should implement multifaceted security measures, including email filtering, employee training, and intrusion detection systems, to defend against targeted campaigns. Vigilance is essential, as attackers continue to refine their tactics and employ increasingly sophisticated methods. In summary, social engineering in targeted campaigns is a persistent and evolving threat in the realm of cybersecurity. Attackers leverage personalized approaches, detailed research, and emotional manipulation to exploit the vulnerabilities of their chosen victims. Recognizing the tactics employed in these campaigns and fostering a cybersecurity-conscious culture is crucial for individuals and organizations seeking to defend against them.

Chapter 4: Network Mapping and Fingerprinting

In the world of cybersecurity, advanced network mapping and enumeration techniques play a critical role in understanding and securing complex networks. These techniques are essential for identifying vulnerabilities, potential attack vectors, and hidden assets within an organization's infrastructure. Network mapping, in its essence, is the process of discovering and documenting the structure of a network. It involves identifying devices, systems, and their interconnections, allowing administrators to create a visual representation of the network's topology. This representation serves as a valuable tool for network management, troubleshooting, and, most importantly, security assessment. Advanced network mapping techniques go beyond basic network discovery tools. They are designed to provide a comprehensive view of the network, including its physical and logical aspects. One of the fundamental aspects of advanced network mapping is active scanning. Unlike passive techniques that rely on observing network traffic, active scanning involves sending probe packets to devices on the network to elicit responses. These responses provide information about the target devices, such as their IP addresses, open ports, and sometimes even specific software versions. Advanced network mapping tools can perform a wide range of active scanning techniques, including TCP and UDP port scanning, ICMP probing, and OS fingerprinting. OS fingerprinting, in particular, is a valuable technique for identifying the operating systems running on target devices. This information helps attackers and defenders alike understand the potential vulnerabilities associated with specific OS versions. Additionally, advanced network mapping tools can employ banner grabbing, a technique that retrieves banners or service identification strings from network services. These banners often reveal details about the software running on open ports, further aiding in vulnerability assessment. Enumeration, on the other hand, is the process of extracting information about network resources. It goes beyond mapping and delves deeper into identifying services, users, shares, and other valuable assets. Enumeration often occurs after network mapping, as the initial map provides a foundation for the enumeration process. A common enumeration technique is querying network services for information. For example, querying DNS servers can reveal hostnames and IP addresses associated with the network. Enumerating network shares can expose sensitive files and directories accessible to authenticated users. Another critical aspect of advanced enumeration is the use of scripting languages or automated tools to gather information from network services. These scripts can retrieve information from services such as SNMP (Simple Network Management Protocol), LDAP (Lightweight Directory Access Protocol), and SMB (Server Message Block). SNMP enumeration can provide insights into network devices, their configurations, and potential vulnerabilities. LDAP enumeration can reveal user account information, group memberships, and organizational structures. SMB enumeration can expose shared resources, user accounts, and system information. To enhance the effectiveness of network mapping and enumeration, cybersecurity professionals often use frameworks and methodologies. One widely adopted framework is the Open Source Security Testing Methodology Manual (OSSTMM), which provides guidelines for network reconnaissance and enumeration. Another is the Penetration Testing Execution Standard (PTES), which outlines a comprehensive methodology for conducting penetration tests, including network mapping and enumeration. In the context of ethical hacking and penetration testing, advanced network mapping and enumeration are essential phases that lay the groundwork for identifying potential vulnerabilities and developing an attack strategy. However, these techniques must be used responsibly and ethically, following legal and regulatory requirements. Unauthorized network scanning and enumeration can be illegal and may result in severe consequences. In summary, advanced network mapping and enumeration techniques are vital components of cybersecurity and penetration testing. They provide a deeper understanding of network structures, vulnerabilities, and assets, allowing organizations to enhance their security posture and defend against potential threats. When used responsibly and in compliance with legal and ethical standards, these techniques are valuable tools for securing modern networks. In the ever-evolving landscape of cybersecurity, fingerprinting and profiling network assets emerge as indispensable techniques for securing digital infrastructures. These techniques are like a detective's magnifying glass, allowing cybersecurity professionals to scrutinize and understand every detail of the network's components. Fingerprinting, in essence, is the process of identifying specific attributes or characteristics that make a network asset unique. It is akin to recognizing someone by their distinctive features and behavior. Network assets, including devices, operating systems, applications, and even users, possess unique fingerprints that can be used for identification. Fingerprinting can be both active and passive, depending on whether it involves interaction with the target asset. Active fingerprinting typically entails sending requests to a network asset and analyzing its responses. One well-known example is the use of the Internet Control Message Protocol (ICMP) echo requests, commonly known as "ping," to determine whether a host is reachable and gather information about its responsiveness. Another active fingerprinting technique involves sending specific requests to a service or application and analyzing the responses. For example, Simple Network Management Protocol (SNMP) queries can reveal details about network devices, while banner grabbing can extract information about the software running on open ports. On the other hand, passive fingerprinting relies on observing network traffic and analyzing patterns and characteristics. It doesn't involve direct interaction with the target asset, making it less intrusive. One of the most notable passive fingerprinting techniques is passive OS fingerprinting. This method involves analyzing network packets and their characteristics to determine the operating system of a remote host. It leverages unique patterns and quirks in how different operating systems construct and respond to network packets. Passive fingerprinting can also be applied to other network assets, such as web applications and services, by analyzing their behaviors and responses. Profiling, on the other hand, takes fingerprinting a step further by creating a detailed profile of a network asset. It's akin to building a comprehensive dossier about an individual, collecting information about their characteristics, behavior, and history. Network asset profiling aims to gather extensive data about the asset's attributes, vulnerabilities, and potential weaknesses. This information is invaluable for cybersecurity professionals, as it helps in assessing the security posture of network assets and identifying potential threats. One crucial aspect of profiling is vulnerability profiling, which involves identifying known vulnerabilities associated with specific assets. For example, a vulnerability profiling scan may reveal that a particular web server version is susceptible to a known exploit. By understanding these vulnerabilities, organizations can prioritize patching and mitigation efforts to reduce security risks. User profiling is another significant aspect of asset profiling. It involves gathering data about user behaviors, access privileges, and usage patterns. Understanding user profiles can help organizations detect unusual or suspicious activities that may indicate a security breach or insider threat. Profiling can also extend to application profiling, where detailed information about software applications and services is collected. This includes versions, configurations, and even the presence of customizations or third-party plugins. Application profiling is crucial for identifying security weaknesses and ensuring that applications are up to date with the latest security patches. Incorporating fingerprinting and profiling into a comprehensive cybersecurity strategy is essential in today's threat landscape. By understanding the unique attributes and behaviors of network assets, organizations can proactively identify and mitigate security risks. These techniques empower cybersecurity professionals to make informed decisions about asset security, vulnerability management, and incident response. However, it's crucial to approach fingerprinting and profiling with ethical considerations in mind. Respecting privacy and compliance with legal regulations are paramount when collecting and analyzing data about network assets and users. In summary, fingerprinting and profiling network assets are invaluable practices for modern cybersecurity. They enable organizations to identify and understand the unique characteristics and vulnerabilities of their digital infrastructure. When conducted responsibly and ethically, fingerprinting and profiling contribute significantly to strengthening an organization's security posture and defending against evolving threats.

Chapter 5: Zero-Day Vulnerability Research

Zero-day exploits, the term itself carries an air of mystery and intrigue, often conjuring images of clandestine hackers operating on the fringes of cyberspace. In the realm of cybersecurity, a zero-day exploit represents a potent weapon—one that targets a vulnerability that is entirely unknown to the software or hardware vendor. This critical unknown factor is what makes zero-day exploits so formidable and highly sought after by malicious actors. To understand the significance of zero-day exploits, we must first delve into the nature of software vulnerabilities. In the digital landscape, vulnerabilities are akin to cracks in the armor of software applications, operating systems, or even hardware. They are the weak points that can be exploited by attackers to gain unauthorized access, compromise data, or execute malicious code. Software vulnerabilities can arise due to coding errors, design flaws, or unforeseen interactions within complex systems. As software evolves, new vulnerabilities can inadvertently emerge, creating a perpetual cat-and-mouse game between developers and hackers. The discovery of a vulnerability often follows a typical trajectory. First, it may be identified by researchers, either from within the organization that develops the software or by independent security experts. These individuals may notice unexpected behavior, unexpected crashes, or other anomalies that hint at an underlying problem. Once a potential vulnerability is suspected, researchers begin to dig deeper, often employing techniques like reverse engineering or fuzz testing to pinpoint the exact cause. When they succeed in isolating the vulnerability, it's typically disclosed responsibly to the software vendor. This responsible disclosure process involves alerting the vendor, providing them with details about the vulnerability, and giving them a reasonable amount of time to develop and release a patch or fix. In an ideal scenario, this collaboration between researchers and vendors leads to improved security and the protection of users from potential threats. However, the story takes a different turn when we talk about zero-day exploits. A zero-day vulnerability is one for which there is no known fix or patch available. It's a security flaw that exists "in the wild," meaning that attackers are already aware of it and are actively exploiting it. This is where the term "zero-day" comes from; it represents the number of days that defenders have had to prepare for the vulnerability. The discovery of a zero-day vulnerability often starts with malicious actors, not well-intentioned security researchers. These attackers, often state-sponsored groups or cybercriminals, are constantly on the lookout for vulnerabilities they can exploit to further their objectives. When they discover a zero-day vulnerability, they typically keep it a closely guarded secret, ensuring that it remains a valuable asset in their cyber arsenal. Why is a zero-day exploit so coveted in the world of cyber warfare and cybercrime? The answer lies in the element of surprise and the potential for maximum impact. Since no one, not even the software vendor, is aware of the vulnerability, there are no defenses in place to mitigate the threat. This allows attackers to launch highly effective and damaging attacks. For example, a zero-day exploit targeting a popular web browser could be used to compromise thousands or even millions of users before a patch is developed and deployed. The implications of zero-day exploits are far-reaching and significant. They pose a substantial risk to individuals, organizations, and even nations. The potential consequences range from data breaches and financial losses to espionage, critical infrastructure disruption, and even acts of cyber warfare. To mitigate the impact of zero-day exploits, organizations must adopt a proactive and multi-faceted approach to cybersecurity. This includes implementing robust security measures, such as intrusion detection systems, firewalls, and endpoint protection, to detect and block malicious activities. Regular security assessments and penetration testing can help identify vulnerabilities before attackers do. Moreover, organizations should stay informed about emerging threats and zero-day vulnerabilities by participating in information-sharing initiatives and monitoring security advisories from trusted sources. However, it's essential to recognize that defending against zero-day exploits is an ongoing challenge. There will always be a degree of uncertainty and risk associated with these vulnerabilities. In some cases, organizations may consider the use of threat intelligence services to gain insights into potential zero-day threats actively exploited in the wild. This information can help security teams stay one step ahead of attackers. Additionally, software vendors play a crucial role in the fight against zero-day exploits. They must be committed to promptly addressing and patching vulnerabilities when they are responsibly disclosed. Timely and effective patch management can significantly reduce the window of opportunity for attackers to exploit zero-day vulnerabilities. In summary, zero-day exploits are the enigmatic and potent weapons of the cybersecurity landscape. Their discovery and implications highlight the constant cat-and-mouse game between defenders and attackers in the digital realm. While the risk of zero-day exploits cannot be eliminated entirely, organizations can reduce their exposure by adopting robust security measures, staying informed, and collaborating with software vendors and the broader security community. Vulnerability analysis and exploit development are integral components of modern cybersecurity, playing a crucial role in identifying, understanding, and mitigating security weaknesses. In the ever-evolving landscape of digital threats, the process of vulnerability analysis serves as a proactive and defensive measure. It involves the systematic examination of software, hardware, or network systems to uncover potential vulnerabilities that could be exploited by malicious actors. Vulnerability analysis encompasses a wide range of activities, from identifying coding errors and configuration flaws to analyzing system architecture and conducting penetration testing. The ultimate goal is to discover and assess vulnerabilities before they can be leveraged by cybercriminals, state-sponsored actors, or hacktivists. Understanding vulnerabilities is the first step towards effective cybersecurity. For security professionals, this means analyzing software and hardware systems, probing for weaknesses, and assessing the potential impact of exploitation. Such analyses can reveal critical insights into a system's security posture, enabling organizations to prioritize and address vulnerabilities based on their severity and potential impact. Exploit development, on the other hand, focuses on the offensive side of cybersecurity. It involves the creation of specific techniques, scripts, or pieces of code that can take advantage of vulnerabilities to compromise a system. Exploits can target various components, such as operating systems, applications, or network protocols, and they come in various forms, including buffer overflows, code injection, privilege escalation, and more. These offensive capabilities are often developed by security researchers, penetration testers, or, regrettably, by malicious hackers with malicious intent. The ethical aspect of exploit development is a critical consideration, as it can be used for both defensive and offensive purposes. In the hands of ethical hackers or security professionals, exploits can serve as tools for assessing and strengthening the security of systems, revealing weaknesses that need to be addressed. However, when wielded by malicious actors, these same exploits can lead to data breaches, system compromises, and widespread cyberattacks. The development of exploits is a complex and multifaceted process that requires a deep understanding of the targeted systems and their vulnerabilities. It typically involves several stages, starting with vulnerability discovery and analysis. Once a vulnerability is identified, researchers must create a proof-of-concept (PoC) exploit to demonstrate that it can be successfully exploited. This PoC is a critical step in understanding the vulnerability's impact and validating its existence. Next, researchers work on creating a reliable and effective exploit code that can be deployed in real-world scenarios. This entails crafting the code to work consistently and predictably, even across different system configurations. During this phase, security professionals must also consider evasion techniques to bypass security mechanisms such as intrusion detection systems and antivirus solutions. The final stage of exploit development involves testing and validation. This phase is crucial to ensure that the exploit behaves as expected and achieves its objectives. Security researchers conduct extensive testing to verify the reliability, stability, and stealthiness of the exploit, as well as to ensure it does not cause unintended consequences. It is essential to note that the development of exploits for ethical purposes, such as penetration testing or red teaming, requires strict adherence to legal and ethical guidelines. Responsible security professionals prioritize the safety and security of systems, data, and individuals during the testing process. This includes obtaining proper authorization and informed consent, as well as carefully considering the potential impact of their actions on the target organization. Furthermore, exploit development is an ongoing and dynamic field. As software and hardware evolve, new vulnerabilities surface, and existing ones may be patched or mitigated. This constant flux necessitates continuous research, innovation, and adaptation in the world of exploit development. The knowledge and skills required for vulnerability analysis and exploit development are highly specialized and sought after in the cybersecurity industry. Ethical hackers and security professionals with expertise in this area play a critical role in securing digital infrastructures, helping organizations stay ahead of potential threats. In summary, vulnerability analysis and exploit development are two sides of the cybersecurity coin—one focused on identifying and addressing weaknesses, and the other on understanding and leveraging those weaknesses for defensive or offensive purposes. When carried out responsibly and ethically, these activities contribute to a safer and more resilient digital ecosystem, protecting individuals, organizations, and society as a whole from cyber threats.

Chapter 6: Exploiting Advanced Web Application Vulnerabilities

In the realm of web application security, going beyond the well-known OWASP (Open Web Application Security Project) Top Ten vulnerabilities is essential to truly fortify your web applications against advanced threats. While the OWASP Top Ten provides a foundational understanding of common vulnerabilities, it's crucial to recognize that attackers are continually evolving their techniques to exploit less well-known weaknesses. This chapter will delve into some of these advanced web application vulnerabilities, shedding light on their intricacies and exploring effective mitigation strategies. One such advanced vulnerability is Cross-Site Request Forgery (CSRF), often referred to as "session riding" or "one-click attack." Unlike the more common Cross-Site Scripting (XSS) or SQL Injection vulnerabilities, CSRF attacks don't rely on injecting malicious code into a web application. Instead, they manipulate a user's authenticated session to perform unintended actions without their consent. Imagine an attacker crafting a malicious email with an image tag pointing to a URL that performs a money transfer when loaded. If a user, while logged into their banking application, views this email, the request to transfer funds could be executed without their knowledge. To mitigate CSRF attacks, developers should implement anti-CSRF tokens within their web applications. These tokens are unique to each user session and must be submitted with sensitive requests, ensuring that only authorized actions are permitted. Another advanced vulnerability is Insecure Deserialization, which occurs when an application processes serialized data from an untrusted source. Serialization is the process of converting an object into a byte stream, often used for data storage or transmission. If an attacker can manipulate the serialized data and the application lacks proper input validation, they can execute arbitrary code. Mitigating insecure deserialization requires careful input validation and secure deserialization libraries. Input validation ensures that only valid and expected data is processed, while using secure deserialization libraries can help reduce the risk of code execution. Next on our journey through advanced web application vulnerabilities is Business Logic Flaws. These vulnerabilities are particularly challenging because they are often specific to a particular application and its intended functionality. Attackers exploit business logic flaws to subvert the intended workflow and carry out malicious activities. For example, an e-commerce site may have a flaw that allows users to purchase items at a fraction of their actual cost. Mitigating business logic flaws necessitates a thorough understanding of the application's intended functionality and rigorous testing. Regularly reviewing and testing an application's logic for inconsistencies or unauthorized actions can help uncover and rectify such vulnerabilities. Now, let's explore Insecure Direct Object References (IDOR), another advanced vulnerability. IDOR occurs when an attacker can manipulate references to internal implementation objects, such as files, databases, or resources. For example, a web application may use predictable numeric IDs to access user-specific data. If an attacker changes the ID in a URL or form submission, they could access another user's data. To mitigate IDOR vulnerabilities, implement proper authorization checks and ensure that user inputs are validated against access controls. Additionally, consider using indirect references, such as unique tokens, rather than direct object references. File Upload vulnerabilities also pose a significant risk, allowing attackers to upload malicious files or scripts to a server. This can lead to various attacks, such as code execution, denial of service, or data leakage. Mitigating file upload vulnerabilities requires strict validation of file types and content, storing uploaded files in a separate, non-executable directory, and applying proper access controls. Server-Side Request Forgery (SSRF) is another advanced vulnerability that involves an attacker manipulating a server's requests to access internal resources. Attackers can use SSRF to perform reconnaissance on internal networks, exfiltrate data, or carry out attacks on other systems. To mitigate SSRF vulnerabilities, it's essential to validate and sanitize user-provided URLs, implement whitelists of allowed hosts, and restrict the server's access to sensitive resources. Lastly, let's discuss XML External Entity (XXE) attacks, a type of vulnerability that affects applications parsing XML input. Attackers can exploit XXE vulnerabilities to read arbitrary files, carry out denial-of-service attacks, or execute malicious code on the server. Mitigating XXE vulnerabilities involves disabling external entity expansion, using secure XML parsers, and filtering or sanitizing user-supplied XML inputs. In summary, web application security extends far beyond the OWASP Top Ten vulnerabilities. To safeguard your applications against advanced threats, it's crucial to understand and address less common vulnerabilities like CSRF, insecure deserialization, business logic flaws, IDOR, file upload issues, SSRF, and XXE. By incorporating robust security practices, rigorous testing, and continuous vigilance, you can enhance the security of your web applications and protect sensitive data from advanced attackers. In the ever-evolving landscape of web application security, advanced techniques for exploiting vulnerabilities are continuously emerging. These techniques are employed by attackers to bypass traditional security measures and compromise web applications. Understanding these advanced exploitation methods is crucial for both security professionals and developers, as it allows for more effective defense and mitigation. One of the advanced exploitation techniques is known as "Parameter Tampering" or "Request Parameter Manipulation." In this attack, an attacker manipulates input parameters sent to the web application, aiming to modify its behavior or gain unauthorized access. For instance, an e-commerce website may use URL parameters to specify the quantity and price of products. An attacker can manipulate these parameters to reduce the price to zero or increase the quantity significantly, potentially causing financial loss to the business. To defend against parameter tampering, developers should validate input parameters and enforce strict access controls to ensure that users can only modify their data within legitimate bounds. Another advanced exploitation technique is "HTTP Verb Tampering" or "HTTP Method Manipulation." Web applications typically use HTTP methods like GET, POST, PUT, and DELETE to perform different actions. An attacker may attempt to change the HTTP method of a request to gain unauthorized access or execute unintended actions. For example, if an application restricts access to a particular resource using POST requests, an attacker may try to use a GET request to bypass the security controls. To mitigate HTTP verb tampering, developers should enforce strict access controls based on the intended HTTP methods and reject any unauthorized method changes. "Server-Side Template Injection" (SSTI) is another advanced web application vulnerability that attackers exploit. SSTI occurs when an application allows user input to control server-side template expressions. This can lead to remote code execution, allowing attackers to execute arbitrary code on the server. For instance, if a web application uses templates for rendering dynamic content and doesn't properly validate user inputs, an attacker can inject malicious code into the template, potentially compromising the server. To protect against SSTI, developers should avoid using user input directly in templates and utilize secure templating engines that prevent code execution from untrusted sources. Next, let's delve into "HTTP Parameter Pollution" (HPP), an advanced exploitation technique that occurs when an attacker manipulates multiple parameters in a single HTTP request. HPP can lead to various issues, such as incorrect data processing, privilege escalation, or even security bypass. For example, if an application allows a user to specify multiple parameters in a single request, an attacker could manipulate them to perform unauthorized actions. To prevent HPP attacks, developers should carefully validate and parse HTTP request parameters and reject requests with duplicate or conflicting parameters. "DOM-Based Cross-Site Scripting" (DOM-XSS) is a sophisticated exploitation technique in which an attacker manipulates the Document Object Model (DOM) of a web page to inject malicious scripts. Unlike traditional Cross-Site Scripting (XSS) attacks, which involve the server reflecting malicious scripts back to the client, DOM-XSS attacks occur entirely on the client-side. For example, an attacker could manipulate the DOM by injecting malicious JavaScript into a web page's URL, which, when executed by the victim's browser, can steal sensitive information or perform other malicious actions. Defending against DOM-XSS requires implementing secure coding practices, including proper input validation and encoding, as well as regularly auditing client-side scripts for vulnerabilities. "Blind SQL Injection" is an advanced exploitation technique used to extract information from a database by injecting SQL queries without directly observing the results. In a blind SQL injection attack, the attacker sends malicious SQL queries to the application's database, and the application's response indirectly reveals information about the database's structure or content. For example, an attacker may exploit a login page vulnerability to extract user credentials from the database without directly seeing the data. To protect against blind SQL injection, developers should use parameterized queries, input validation, and output encoding to prevent malicious SQL injection attempts. Lastly, let's explore "HTTP Response Smuggling," an advanced technique used by attackers to manipulate the interpretation of HTTP responses between a proxy server and a web application. This technique can lead to various attacks, including cache poisoning and session hijacking. To perform HTTP response smuggling, an attacker sends a crafted request to a vulnerable web application that causes discrepancies in how the request is parsed by the web server and the proxy server. As a result, the attacker can control the interpretation of responses and potentially manipulate the behavior of the proxy server. To defend against HTTP response smuggling, developers should implement security measures like request validation, ensuring consistency between the web server and proxy server configurations. In summary, understanding advanced exploitation techniques for web application vulnerabilities is essential for building robust and secure web applications. Developers and security professionals must remain vigilant, employ secure coding practices, and implement effective security controls to mitigate these advanced threats effectively. By staying informed about emerging exploitation methods and continuously improving security measures, organizations can protect their web applications and data from evolving threats in the digital landscape.

Chapter 7: Cryptography and Data Protection

In the world of cybersecurity, advanced cryptographic algorithms and techniques play a pivotal role in safeguarding sensitive data and communications. These cryptographic methods go beyond the basics, offering enhanced security against sophisticated attacks. Let's delve into some of these advanced cryptographic techniques and their significance in today's digital landscape.

One crucial concept in advanced cryptography is "Quantum-Safe Cryptography." With the rise of quantum computing, traditional cryptographic algorithms like RSA and ECC face the risk of being broken by powerful quantum computers. Quantum-safe cryptography, also known as post-quantum cryptography, aims to develop algorithms and techniques that can withstand attacks from quantum computers. These algorithms use mathematical problems that are believed to be hard even for quantum computers to solve, ensuring long-term security for encrypted data.

Another advanced cryptographic technique is "Homomorphic Encryption." Homomorphic encryption allows computations to be performed on encrypted data without decrypting it first. This means that data can remain confidential even when it's being processed. This is particularly valuable in scenarios where privacy is paramount, such as medical research or confidential data analysis. Companies and organizations can perform calculations on sensitive data without exposing it, maintaining the highest level of security.

"Zero-Knowledge Proofs" are cryptographic protocols that enable one party (the prover) to prove to another party (the verifier) that they possess certain knowledge without revealing what that knowledge is. This technique has profound implications for privacy and security. For example, it can be used in password authentication without transmitting the actual password. Instead, a zero-knowledge proof can be used to confirm that the user knows the password without disclosing it, reducing the risk of password leaks.

Blockchain technology relies heavily on advanced cryptography. "Elliptic Curve Digital Signature Algorithm" (ECDSA) is a widely used cryptographic algorithm in blockchain networks like Bitcoin and Ethereum. ECDSA provides a secure way to create digital signatures, which are essential for verifying transactions and maintaining the integrity of the blockchain. Without advanced cryptographic techniques like ECDSA, the security of blockchain-based systems would be compromised.

For secure communication over untrusted networks, "Post-Quantum Key Exchange" protocols come into play. These protocols ensure that cryptographic keys can be exchanged securely even in the presence of quantum computers. Post-quantum key exchange methods are essential for maintaining the confidentiality and integrity of data transmitted over the internet, especially as the threat of quantum computing looms on the horizon.

As we navigate the era of the Internet of Things (IoT), "Secure Device Authentication" becomes increasingly crucial. Advanced cryptographic techniques are employed to ensure that IoT devices can securely authenticate themselves to networks and other devices. This prevents unauthorized access and potential security breaches in IoT ecosystems, safeguarding sensitive data and critical infrastructure.

In the realm of secure messaging, "End-to-End Encryption" (E2EE) is a well-known advanced cryptographic technique. E2EE ensures that only the sender and intended recipient can decrypt and read the messages. Even service providers or intermediaries cannot access the content of the messages, ensuring utmost privacy and security in communication.

"Fully Homomorphic Encryption" (FHE) is an advanced cryptographic scheme that takes homomorphic encryption to the next level. While homomorphic encryption allows limited operations on encrypted data, FHE enables arbitrary computations on encrypted data. This has profound implications for secure data processing, especially in scenarios where sensitive data needs to be outsourced to the cloud while remaining encrypted and confidential.

In today's digital landscape, securing data at rest is as critical as securing data in transit. "Advanced Encryption Standard" (AES) with larger key sizes, like AES-256, is widely used to encrypt data at rest. This robust encryption algorithm ensures that even if an adversary gains access to encrypted data, deciphering it without the encryption key remains computationally infeasible.

In the context of authentication and access control, "Multi-Factor Authentication" (MFA) combines something you know (like a password) with something you have (like a smartphone or hardware token) to enhance security. Cryptographic techniques are employed to ensure the integrity and confidentiality of the authentication process. MFA has become a standard practice in enhancing the security of online accounts and systems.

As we explore advanced cryptographic algorithms and techniques, it's essential to recognize that cryptography is an ever-evolving field. New threats and vulnerabilities emerge, and cryptography must adapt to address them. The use of cryptographic techniques is not limited to securing data and communications; it extends to various domains, including finance, healthcare, national security, and beyond.

In summary, advanced cryptographic algorithms and techniques are the cornerstone of modern cybersecurity. They provide the means to protect sensitive data, secure communications, and ensure the privacy and integrity of information in an increasingly digital world. As technology advances, so too must cryptography, and staying at the forefront of these advancements is paramount for individuals, organizations, and societies to maintain their security and privacy in a digital age.

In the realm of cybersecurity, secure data storage and transmission are paramount concerns that shape how individuals, organizations, and governments protect their sensitive information and communications. As our world becomes increasingly digitized, the need to safeguard data from cyber threats and unauthorized access has never been more critical.

When we discuss secure data storage, we delve into the techniques and practices that ensure data remains protected, whether it's at rest or in transit. Let's explore the importance of secure data storage and transmission in today's interconnected world.

Secure data storage begins with encryption, a fundamental practice that converts readable data into an unreadable format using complex algorithms and cryptographic keys. Encryption safeguards data at rest, ensuring that even if someone gains physical access to the storage medium, they cannot decipher the information without the encryption key. One widely adopted encryption method is "Full Disk Encryption" (FDE), which encrypts the entire storage device, whether it's a hard drive, solid-state drive, or other storage media. FDE provides a strong layer of protection, making it challenging for unauthorized parties to access or extract data from the device.

For cloud-based storage solutions, "Client-Side Encryption" allows users to encrypt their data on their own devices before uploading it to the cloud. This means that cloud service providers cannot access or view the content of the stored data, maintaining user privacy and control.

In the realm of data transmission, securing information as it travels across networks and the internet is crucial. "Transport Layer Security" (TLS) and its predecessor, "Secure Sockets Layer" (SSL), are cryptographic protocols that establish secure communication channels between two parties, such as a web browser and a web server. TLS ensures that data transmitted over the internet remains confidential and cannot be intercepted or tampered with by attackers.

Another critical aspect of secure data transmission is "End-to-End Encryption" (E2EE). E2EE ensures that data remains encrypted throughout its journey from the sender to the recipient. Even service providers and intermediaries cannot access the content of the data, providing the highest level of privacy and security in communication.

In addition to encryption, secure data transmission involves secure protocols and authentication mechanisms. "Secure File Transfer Protocols" (SFTP) and "Secure Shell" (SSH) are examples of protocols that ensure secure data transfer by encrypting data and verifying the identities of the communicating parties.

To enhance security further, "Virtual Private Networks" (VPNs) create secure and encrypted tunnels for data transmission over public networks. VPNs are widely used to protect sensitive data from eavesdropping and maintain privacy, especially when accessing the internet from untrusted networks.

In secure data storage, "Access Control" mechanisms play a pivotal role in ensuring that only authorized individuals or entities can access data. Access control includes user authentication, authorization, and auditing. Usernames, passwords, biometrics, and multi-factor authentication (MFA) are common authentication methods that prevent unauthorized access to data.

Authorization specifies what actions users or systems are allowed to perform once authenticated. It ensures that individuals can only access the data and perform operations for which they have permission. Auditing tracks who accesses data and what actions they take, providing accountability and a record of data access for security and compliance purposes.

In the modern era, where data is often distributed across various devices and locations, "Data Backup and Redundancy" are essential components of secure data storage. Regular backups ensure that data can be restored in the event of data loss due to hardware failure, data corruption, or cyberattacks.

Secure data storage is not limited to traditional data centers but extends to "Distributed Ledger Technologies" (DLT) such as blockchain. Blockchain's decentralized and immutable nature ensures data integrity and security, making it suitable for applications like cryptocurrency transactions and supply chain management.

Moreover, "Homomorphic Encryption" is an advanced cryptographic technique that allows computations to be performed on encrypted data without decrypting it. This has significant implications for secure data processing and analysis, as organizations can perform operations on sensitive data without exposing it.

In the context of secure data transmission, the "Internet of Things" (IoT) presents unique challenges. IoT devices often transmit sensitive data over networks, making encryption and security protocols crucial to protect this data from interception and manipulation.

Furthermore, "Secure Data Erasure" practices ensure that data is securely and permanently removed from storage devices when it is no longer needed. This prevents data breaches and unauthorized access to sensitive information, especially when devices are decommissioned or recycled.

In summary, secure data storage and transmission are fundamental pillars of cybersecurity in our digital age. Encryption, access control, authentication, and backup strategies are essential components of protecting data at rest. Meanwhile, encryption, secure protocols, and privacy-enhancing technologies like VPNs and E2EE ensure secure data transmission.

As our reliance on digital data continues to grow, so too will the importance of secure data storage and transmission. Whether it's safeguarding personal information, protecting intellectual property, or ensuring national security, the principles and practices of secure data handling will remain central to our digital lives.

Chapter 8: Nation-State Level Reconnaissance Tactics

In the ever-evolving landscape of cybersecurity, one of the most significant and complex challenges that governments, organizations, and individuals face is the threat posed by nation-state actors. These are not your typical hackers or cybercriminals; instead, they are often well-funded, highly skilled, and backed by the resources of a nation-state, such as a government or intelligence agency.

Nation-state threat actors, also known as Advanced Persistent Threats (APTs), operate with strategic objectives that go beyond financial gain or personal motives. They are motivated by geopolitical interests, espionage, military advantage, or economic competition. Understanding their tactics is essential for building effective defenses against them.

One of the defining characteristics of nation-state threat actors is their persistence. They are not looking for quick financial gain; they are willing to invest significant time and resources to achieve their goals. They often employ a range of tactics, techniques, and procedures (TTPs) to maintain access to target networks for extended periods, sometimes years.

One of the most common tactics employed by nation-state actors is spear-phishing. Unlike mass phishing campaigns that target a wide audience, spear-phishing involves crafting highly customized and convincing emails to target specific individuals or organizations. These emails often contain malicious attachments or links designed to compromise the recipient's system.

Another tactic utilized by nation-state actors is watering hole attacks. In these attacks, threat actors identify websites frequently visited by their targets, such as government or industry-related sites. They then compromise these websites, injecting malware into them. When a target visits one of these infected sites, their system can be compromised without their knowledge.

Supply chain attacks are another favored tactic of nation-state actors. They target software vendors, hardware manufacturers, or service providers in the supply chain of a target organization. By compromising a trusted entity, attackers can gain access to their customers' networks. This tactic was famously demonstrated in the SolarWinds breach, where a nation-state actor compromised a software update to gain access to multiple government and private-sector networks.

To maintain persistence within a target network, nation-state actors often use backdoors and implants. These are pieces of malicious software that provide remote access and control over compromised systems. They are carefully designed to avoid detection and can be tailored to the specific target environment.

Advanced malware is another tool in the arsenal of nation-state threat actors. This includes highly sophisticated and evasive malware strains that are difficult to detect and remove. These malware variants often have capabilities for data exfiltration, reconnaissance, and lateral movement within a network.

Lateral movement is a crucial tactic for these threat actors once they gain an initial foothold. They move laterally within a network to explore and compromise additional systems, seeking valuable data or expanding their influence. They use techniques like pass-the-hash attacks, privilege escalation, and lateral traversal to achieve this.

Nation-state actors are also known for their use of zero-day vulnerabilities. These are software vulnerabilities that are unknown to the vendor and, therefore, lack patches or fixes.

These threat actors may discover or purchase zero-day vulnerabilities to gain a significant advantage in their operations.

Another hallmark of nation-state actors is the use of sophisticated command and control (C2) infrastructure. They establish resilient and covert C2 channels to communicate with compromised systems. These channels often use encryption and mimic legitimate traffic to avoid detection.

In addition to traditional cyber tactics, nation-state actors have been known to engage in supply chain manipulation. This involves compromising the hardware or software components of a target organization's infrastructure. For example, they might insert hardware-level implants into servers or routers before they reach the target.

Cyber-espionage is a primary motive for many nation-state threat actors. They seek to steal sensitive information, intellectual property, or government secrets. Espionage can provide them with valuable insights, competitive advantages, or diplomatic leverage.

In some cases, nation-state actors engage in destructive cyberattacks. These attacks are designed to disrupt or damage critical infrastructure, such as power grids or financial systems. They can have severe consequences and may lead to geopolitical tensions or conflicts.

Attributing cyberattacks to specific nation-state actors is challenging but essential. Various indicators, such as malware signatures, infrastructure, and tactics, can help cybersecurity experts identify the likely origin of an attack. However, false flags and obfuscation techniques make accurate attribution a complex task.

To defend against nation-state threat actors, organizations must adopt a comprehensive cybersecurity strategy. This includes continuous monitoring for suspicious activities, threat intelligence sharing, employee training to recognize phishing attempts, and a robust incident response plan.

In summary, nation-state threat actors represent a formidable challenge in the world of cybersecurity. Their tactics are characterized by sophistication, persistence, and a range of advanced techniques. Understanding their methods is crucial for organizations and governments to protect against these highly motivated and well-resourced adversaries.

Advanced Persistent Threats (APTs) are a category of cybersecurity threat that represent some of the most sophisticated and persistent adversaries in the digital realm. These threats are characterized by their ability to infiltrate and remain undetected within a target network or system for extended periods, often for months or even years.

At the core of APTs is the concept of "persistence." Unlike more opportunistic cyberattacks, APTs are not looking for quick financial gain or immediate disruption. Instead, they have specific objectives, such as stealing sensitive information, conducting espionage, or gaining long-term control over a target's resources.

One of the critical stages in an APT campaign is reconnaissance. This initial phase involves gathering intelligence about the target organization or individual. Reconnaissance helps threat actors understand their target's infrastructure, vulnerabilities, and potential weaknesses that can be exploited later in the attack.

Reconnaissance can take many forms, starting with open-source intelligence (OSINT) gathering. This involves collecting publicly available information about the target, such as corporate websites, social media profiles, and news articles. OSINT provides a valuable starting point for threat actors to identify potential targets within the organization.

In addition to OSINT, APTs often engage in network scanning and probing. This involves scanning a target's network infrastructure for open ports, vulnerabilities, and potential entry points. By identifying vulnerable systems or services, threat actors can plan their attack strategies accordingly.

A common reconnaissance technique used by APTs is social engineering. This involves manipulating individuals within the target organization to divulge sensitive information or provide access credentials. Phishing emails, for example, can be crafted to appear as if they are from a trusted source, enticing recipients to click on malicious links or attachments.

In more advanced cases, APTs may employ "whaling" or "spear-phishing" techniques. These tactics target high-value individuals within the organization, such as executives or system administrators, with highly personalized and convincing messages. The goal is to trick these individuals into taking actions that benefit the attackers.

To further their reconnaissance efforts, APTs may use publicly available data, such as domain registration information, IP address ownership, and historical DNS records. By analyzing this information, threat actors can map the target's digital footprint and identify potential vulnerabilities.

Another critical aspect of reconnaissance for APTs is the identification of key assets and critical data within the target organization. This involves determining what information is most valuable and which systems or servers store this data. Once identified, threat actors can plan their attack vectors accordingly.

In some cases, APTs may leverage insider information or collaborate with insiders within the target organization. Insiders can provide valuable details about the organization's security infrastructure, operational procedures, and even access credentials. This insider knowledge can significantly aid in reconnaissance efforts.

As part of their reconnaissance activities, APTs may also conduct passive monitoring of the target's network traffic. This can help them gather information about the organization's communication patterns, systems in use, and potential vulnerabilities. Passive monitoring is designed to avoid detection and raise fewer suspicion flags.

To maintain stealth during reconnaissance, APTs often employ various evasion techniques, such as IP anonymization, using proxy servers, and employing encrypted communication channels. These tactics make it challenging for defenders to detect their activities or trace them back to their true origins.

In some instances, APTs may go a step further and establish persistent backdoors or implants within the target's network. These backdoors allow attackers to maintain access even if initial entry points are discovered and closed. This persistence is crucial for conducting long-term surveillance or espionage.

In summary, Advanced Persistent Threats (APTs) represent a highly sophisticated and persistent category of cyber threats. Reconnaissance is a crucial phase in APT campaigns, involving the gathering of intelligence about the target organization, its assets, vulnerabilities, and potential entry points. Threat actors employ a variety of techniques, including open-source intelligence (OSINT), network scanning, social engineering, and insider collaboration, to gather the necessary information while maintaining stealth and persistence within the target's environment. Understanding APT reconnaissance tactics is essential for organizations to strengthen their cybersecurity defenses against these formidable adversaries.

Chapter 9: Advanced Data Exfiltration Strategies

Covert data exfiltration techniques are a critical aspect of cybersecurity, both from an offensive and defensive perspective. These techniques involve surreptitiously stealing and transmitting sensitive information from a target system or network without detection. Understanding these methods is essential for organizations seeking to protect their data and assets, as well as for security professionals responsible for identifying and mitigating potential threats.

One common covert data exfiltration technique involves disguising data within seemingly innocuous network traffic. This can be achieved through techniques like steganography, which embeds hidden data within images, audio files, or other media. By manipulating the least significant bits of digital content, attackers can conceal sensitive information within the noise of legitimate traffic. Another method for covert data exfiltration is through the use of covert channels within network protocols. Attackers can manipulate unused or less-monitored fields in network packets to transmit data. This method can be challenging to detect because it doesn't rely on any specific network ports or communication patterns.

DNS tunneling is another covert data exfiltration technique that exploits the Domain Name System (DNS) to transmit data. Attackers create subdomains that encode the stolen information, and these subdomains are resolved by DNS servers. This technique allows attackers to bypass network security measures that may not inspect DNS traffic thoroughly.

In some cases, attackers may employ encryption to exfiltrate data covertly. By encrypting the stolen information, they can make it appear as random or benign traffic, which is less likely to raise suspicion. Decryption keys are held by the attacker or a compromised entity on the receiving end.

Attackers may also use a technique known as "data exfiltration over alternative protocols." This involves transmitting data over protocols not typically associated with data transmission, such as ICMP (Internet Control Message Protocol). By encapsulating stolen data within ICMP packets, attackers can bypass traditional security measures.

Covert data exfiltration can also occur through the exploitation of trusted applications or services. Attackers might use legitimate cloud storage or file-sharing services to store and retrieve stolen data. This method can be challenging to detect since it relies on authorized applications.

Mobile devices can also be used for covert data exfiltration. Attackers may exfiltrate data through smartphones or tablets, leveraging their connectivity to the internet. Mobile devices are often overlooked in corporate security strategies, making them attractive targets for data theft.

Social engineering can play a significant role in covert data exfiltration. Attackers may manipulate employees or other individuals with access to the target network to extract data on their behalf. This can involve tricking individuals into providing access credentials or transferring sensitive files.

In addition to covertly stealing data, attackers must also find ways to maintain access to the compromised system or network. This may involve creating persistent backdoors or malware that allows them to return and continue exfiltrating data over time. Backdoors are often disguised or obfuscated to evade detection.

Detecting covert data exfiltration can be challenging, as attackers continually develop new and sophisticated techniques to evade detection. Security professionals must employ a combination of network monitoring, anomaly detection, and behavioral analysis to identify suspicious patterns of data traffic. Machine learning and artificial intelligence tools can also help recognize unusual patterns of behavior that may indicate covert exfiltration. Preventing covert data exfiltration requires a multi-layered approach to cybersecurity. This includes implementing robust access controls, network monitoring, and intrusion detection systems. Additionally, educating employees about the risks of social engineering and providing training to recognize phishing attempts can help mitigate the threat.

In summary, covert data exfiltration techniques are a critical concern in the world of cybersecurity. Attackers use various methods to steal and transmit sensitive information from target systems or networks without detection. Understanding these techniques is essential for organizations and security professionals seeking to protect their data and assets. Detection and prevention strategies must be multi-faceted and continually updated to address the evolving landscape of covert data exfiltration threats.

Data exfiltration in highly secured environments presents a formidable challenge for both attackers and defenders alike. These environments are characterized by stringent security measures designed to protect sensitive information and prevent unauthorized access. However, determined threat actors continually seek innovative ways to breach these defenses and exfiltrate valuable data.

One of the key challenges in highly secured environments is the presence of robust network and host-based security controls. These controls, such as firewalls, intrusion detection systems, and endpoint security solutions, are designed to monitor and restrict network traffic, making it difficult for attackers to move data out of the network undetected.

To overcome these challenges, attackers often resort to more advanced and covert methods of data exfiltration. They may leverage techniques like domain generation algorithms (DGAs) to establish command and control channels that evade traditional security mechanisms. DGAs generate a large number of domain names, making it challenging for security tools to pinpoint malicious communications.

Additionally, attackers may employ tunneling protocols like SSH or VPNs to create encrypted communication channels, disguising their data exfiltration activities as legitimate traffic. These encrypted channels can bypass deep packet inspection and signature-based detection, making them highly effective in evading security measures.

Steganography, the art of hiding information within seemingly innocuous files or data streams, is another technique used in highly secured environments. Attackers embed sensitive data within images, audio files, or other media, making it virtually indistinguishable from normal content. This covert approach helps them evade detection by security controls.

Infiltrating an organization's insiders is a common tactic used in highly secured environments. Attackers may recruit or compromise employees with privileged access to the network, convincing them to exfiltrate data on their behalf. This insider threat can be difficult to detect because it originates from within the organization.
Highly secured environments often rely on strict access controls and authentication mechanisms, making it challenging for attackers to gain unauthorized access. To circumvent these barriers, attackers may exploit vulnerabilities in third-party applications or conduct spear-phishing campaigns targeting employees with administrative privileges.

Advanced persistent threats (APTs), which are characterized by their persistence and ability to remain undetected for extended periods, are commonly associated with data exfiltration in highly secured environments. APT groups employ a combination of sophisticated techniques, including zero-day exploits, custom malware, and lateral movement within the network, to achieve their objectives.

To detect data exfiltration attempts in these environments, security teams must adopt a multi-layered approach. This includes real-time monitoring of network traffic, log analysis, and behavioral analytics. Machine learning and artificial intelligence can help identify unusual patterns and anomalies indicative of data exfiltration.

Intrusion detection and prevention systems (IDS/IPS) play a crucial role in identifying suspicious activities and blocking data exfiltration attempts. These systems use signature-based and behavioral analysis to detect known attack patterns and deviations from normal network behavior.

Endpoint detection and response (EDR) solutions provide visibility into activities on individual devices, helping security teams identify malicious processes or unauthorized data access. EDR solutions can also facilitate threat hunting, allowing analysts to proactively search for signs of data exfiltration.

User and entity behavior analytics (UEBA) platforms can analyze user and entity behavior patterns to detect anomalies that may indicate insider threats or compromised accounts. By monitoring user activity and correlating it with contextual data, UEBA systems can identify potential data exfiltration attempts.

Effective incident response is critical in highly secured environments. Security teams should have well-defined incident response plans that include isolation of compromised systems, investigation, and remediation steps. Timely response can prevent further data exfiltration and limit the damage caused by a breach.

In summary, data exfiltration in highly secured environments is a complex and evolving challenge.

Attackers employ advanced tactics, techniques, and procedures to bypass security controls and evade detection. Defenders must adopt a multi-layered approach, combining network monitoring, advanced security tools, and vigilant incident response to protect sensitive data in these environments. The constant evolution of threats requires security teams to stay informed, adapt their strategies, and remain prepared to defend against emerging data exfiltration techniques.

Chapter 10: Ethics and Responsibility in Elite Information Gathering

Ethics play a pivotal role in the world of elite information gathering, shaping the boundaries of what is considered acceptable and responsible in the pursuit of intelligence and knowledge. At the heart of this role is the recognition that information can be a powerful tool, and how it is obtained and used can have far-reaching consequences.

In the realm of elite information gathering, individuals and organizations often have access to advanced tools, techniques, and resources that can provide them with a significant advantage. These capabilities can range from cutting-edge technology for cyber espionage to the deployment of human intelligence assets in sensitive environments. However, with great power comes great responsibility, and ethical considerations are central to ensuring that these capabilities are used judiciously.

One of the fundamental ethical principles in elite information gathering is the respect for privacy. The invasion of an individual's or an organization's privacy without just cause or due process is generally regarded as unethical. This respect for privacy extends to the gathering of personal or sensitive information, whether it pertains to individuals, businesses, or governments.

Transparency is another key ethical principle in elite information gathering. Organizations and individuals engaged in this practice must be transparent about their intentions and methods, especially when their actions have the potential to impact the security or privacy of others. Lack of transparency can erode trust and credibility, which are essential in the intelligence-gathering community.

Accountability is closely linked to transparency. Those involved in elite information gathering must be willing to take responsibility for their actions and the consequences that may arise from their pursuit of information. This includes being answerable to ethical oversight, legal authorities, and the public when necessary.

Integrity is a foundational ethical value in the field of elite information gathering. Maintaining the highest standards of honesty and moral character is essential to preserving the credibility and reputation of individuals and organizations involved in intelligence activities. Any compromise of integrity can lead to significant ethical breaches.

Furthermore, the principle of proportionality is crucial when it comes to ethical information gathering. It involves ensuring that the methods used to gather information are proportional to the importance of the information sought and the potential impact of obtaining it. In other words, the ends should justify the means, and excessive or unnecessary intrusion should be avoided.

The principle of minimization is closely related to proportionality. It emphasizes the importance of minimizing the collection and retention of irrelevant or excessive information. Only data that is necessary and directly related to the legitimate intelligence objectives should be gathered and retained.

Human rights and civil liberties are ethical considerations that cannot be overlooked in elite information gathering. Activities that infringe upon the rights and freedoms of individuals or groups are generally regarded as unethical.

Intelligence gathering should never involve activities that violate human rights or undermine the rule of law.

Non-discrimination is another ethical principle that guides the behavior of those engaged in elite information gathering. Discrimination on the basis of race, religion, ethnicity, gender, or any other protected category is considered unethical and unacceptable. Information should be collected and used without bias or prejudice.

Respect for international law and norms is imperative in the realm of elite information gathering. Violations of international law, such as espionage activities that breach the sovereignty of other nations, can have serious diplomatic and ethical repercussions. Adhering to established rules and norms helps maintain stability and prevents unnecessary conflicts.

Ultimately, the role of ethics in elite information gathering is to ensure that the pursuit of intelligence remains within the bounds of moral and legal conduct. While intelligence activities are often conducted in secret and away from the public eye, ethical considerations should always guide decision-making, helping to strike a delicate balance between national security interests and the rights and values of individuals and nations.

In summary, ethics play a foundational role in elite information gathering, shaping the behavior and principles of individuals and organizations engaged in intelligence activities. Upholding ethical values such as respect for privacy, transparency, accountability, integrity, proportionality, and non-discrimination is essential to ensure that information is obtained and used responsibly, without compromising human rights or international norms. Ethical conduct is not only a moral imperative but also a critical aspect of maintaining trust, credibility, and legitimacy in the complex world of elite information gathering.

Responsible disclosure is a fundamental ethical and practical principle in the world of cybersecurity and vulnerability research, emphasizing the importance of reporting security vulnerabilities and weaknesses to the appropriate parties in a responsible and coordinated manner.

When security researchers discover vulnerabilities in software, hardware, or systems, their first instinct might be to publish their findings immediately to raise awareness or gain recognition. However, this approach can lead to serious consequences, including the exploitation of the vulnerabilities by malicious actors before the affected parties have had a chance to patch or mitigate the issues.

Responsible disclosure, also known as coordinated disclosure or responsible vulnerability disclosure (RVD), seeks to strike a balance between the need for transparency and the potential risks associated with public disclosure. The process typically involves several key steps:

Discovery: The first step is identifying and confirming the presence of a vulnerability. This may involve in-depth testing, analysis, and verification to ensure the issue is genuine.

Research: Once a vulnerability is confirmed, security researchers often conduct further research to understand its scope, potential impact, and any possible exploitation scenarios. This information is critical for assessing the severity of the issue.

Notification: After understanding the vulnerability, researchers should contact the affected party or vendor responsible for the software or system. This notification should be made privately, using secure and appropriate channels, to avoid leaking sensitive information prematurely.

Collaboration: Collaboration is a key aspect of responsible disclosure. Researchers and vendors must work together to assess the vulnerability, develop and test patches or mitigations, and establish a timeline for releasing these fixes.

Disclosure Timeline: A mutually agreed-upon timeline for disclosure is established. This timeline balances the need for prompt remediation with the need to give affected parties sufficient time to prepare for the release of vulnerability details.

Public Disclosure: Once the agreed-upon timeline is reached and patches or mitigations are available, the vulnerability details are publicly disclosed. This disclosure typically includes a detailed advisory or report outlining the vulnerability, its impact, and the steps necessary for remediation.

Patch Deployment: Organizations and individuals affected by the vulnerability are encouraged to apply patches or mitigations promptly to protect their systems and data.

Acknowledgment: Researchers who responsibly disclose vulnerabilities are usually credited for their findings. This acknowledgment can take various forms, such as a mention in security advisories or monetary rewards through bug bounty programs.

Responsible disclosure benefits both security researchers and the broader cybersecurity community. It allows researchers to contribute to the improvement of software and systems while minimizing the potential harm that could result from immediate public disclosure. It also promotes a collaborative approach to addressing security issues, fostering better relationships between researchers and vendors.

Collaboration with authorities is another important aspect of responsible disclosure, especially in cases where vulnerabilities have significant implications for national security, critical infrastructure, or public safety. In such situations, researchers may need to work with government agencies or law enforcement to ensure the appropriate response.

Collaboration with authorities typically involves the following steps:

Initial Contact: If a security researcher believes that a vulnerability discovery has implications beyond the scope of traditional responsible disclosure, they may need to initiate contact with relevant authorities. This contact is often made through appropriate legal channels or government agencies responsible for cybersecurity.

Information Sharing: Researchers provide authorities with all relevant information about the vulnerability, its potential impact, and any evidence of malicious exploitation. This information is crucial for assessing the severity and urgency of the situation.

Coordination: Authorities and researchers collaborate to assess the risk and develop a strategy for mitigating the vulnerability. This may involve sharing technical details with government cybersecurity experts.

Response Planning: Based on the assessment, authorities and researchers develop a response plan. This plan may include notifying affected organizations, coordinating the release of patches or mitigations, and monitoring the situation for any signs of malicious activity.

Public Communication: If the situation warrants public communication, authorities and researchers work together to ensure that accurate and timely information is shared with the public and affected parties.

Ongoing Collaboration: Collaboration with authorities is an ongoing process, and researchers may be called upon to provide further assistance or insights as the situation unfolds.

Responsible disclosure and collaboration with authorities are essential components of the cybersecurity landscape. They help ensure that vulnerabilities are addressed in a manner that safeguards both individual security and the broader interests of society. By following ethical guidelines and working together, security researchers and authorities can contribute to a safer and more secure digital environment.

Conclusion

In the ever-evolving landscape of cybersecurity and ethical hacking, knowledge and expertise in reconnaissance are foundational. As we conclude this comprehensive book bundle, "RECONNAISSANCE 101: Footprinting & Information Gathering," we reflect on the journey we've taken through its four enlightening volumes.

Book 1 - "RECONNAISSANCE 101: A Beginner's Guide to Footprinting & Information Gathering" introduced us to the fundamental concepts and techniques of reconnaissance. We embarked on a journey to understand how hackers gather information about target systems, laying the groundwork for ethical hacking skills.

Book 2 - "Mastering Footprinting: Advanced Information Gathering Strategies for Ethical Hackers" elevated our understanding with advanced strategies and tactics. We delved deeper into the intricacies of footprinting, learning how to gather valuable data while remaining undetected.

Book 3 - "The Ethical Hacker's Field Guide to Target Data Acquisition" expanded our horizons, focusing on the critical task of acquiring target-specific data. We explored ethical methods for collecting information that is essential for ethical hackers in assessing vulnerabilities and potential exploits.

Book 4 - "Reconnaissance Pro: The Ultimate Handbook for Elite Information Gatherers" took us to the pinnacle of reconnaissance expertise. We unraveled the secrets of elite information gatherers, gaining insights into techniques that set apart the best in the field.

Together, these four volumes have provided a comprehensive and progressive roadmap for individuals aspiring to become ethical hackers and cybersecurity professionals. They have emphasized the importance of ethical and responsible practices in an era where digital threats are ever-present.

Throughout this bundle, we've emphasized the significance of ethical considerations, responsible disclosure, and collaboration with authorities. These principles underscore the ethical hacker's commitment to making the digital world safer for everyone.

As you close the chapters of this book bundle, remember that your journey in the realm of reconnaissance and ethical hacking is far from over. The ever-evolving nature of technology ensures that there will always be more to learn and explore. Stay curious, stay committed to ethical principles, and continue to hone your skills.

Whether you're a beginner just starting to explore the world of ethical hacking or an experienced professional seeking to enhance your reconnaissance abilities, "RECONNAISSANCE 101: Footprinting & Information Gathering" has equipped you with the knowledge and tools needed to excel in this dynamic field.

In closing, we hope that you find inspiration and motivation within these pages. Your commitment to ethical hacking not only enhances your own expertise but also contributes to a safer digital world for us all. May your ethical hacking journey be filled with continuous learning, responsible practices, and meaningful contributions to the cybersecurity community.

Thank you for joining us on this educational adventure, and we wish you success in all your future endeavors as an ethical hacker and information gatherer.

www.ingramcontent.com/pod-product-compliance
Lightning Source LLC
Chambersburg PA
CBHW071236050326
40690CB00011B/2141